D0812206

Whose War Is It?

Whose War Is It?

How Canada Can Survive in the Post-9/11 World

J. L. Granatstein

HarperCollins Publishers Ltd
A Phyllis Bruce Book

Whose War Is It?

A Phyllis Bruce Book, published by HarperCollins Publishers Ltd.

First Canadian Edition

HarperCollins Publishers Ltd
2 Bloor Street East, 20th Floor
Toronto, Ontario, Canada
M4W 1A8

www.harpercollins.ca

Library and Archives Canada Cataloguing in Publication

Granatstein, J. L., 1939–
Whose war is it? : how Canada can survive in the post-9/11 world / J. L. Granatstein.

A Phyllis Bruce Book.
ISBN-13: 978-0-00-200845-7
ISBN-10: 0-00-200845-9

1. Canada—Politics and government—2006–. 2. National security—Canada—History—21st century. 3. Canada—Military policy. 4. Canada—Foreign relations—United States. 5. United States—Foreign relations—Canada. I. Title.

FC640.G73 2007 971.07'3 C2006-906572-1

HC 9 8 7 6 5 4 3 2 1

Printed and bound in the United States
Set in Janson Text
Design by Sharon Kish

For Elaine, Carole, and Tess,
the ladies in my life

Contents

Preface

My colleague and friend, the historian Michael Bliss, began a recent address by saying he had reached the age and stage in his life and career when he had licence to begin reflecting on the big picture. So have I; indeed, because I'm a few years older than Michael, I have even more reason to offer my reflections.

Hence, this book. Here I write frankly about and examine what I consider to be the key problems that affect Canada's present foreign and defence policies. We are in a war against terror that will affect us even as Canadians hope in vain that it will not. It is Canada's war because we are a First World nation-state firmly within the Western tradition, and in this struggle (which is on the verge of becoming existential) we need to bolster our defences, military and ideological. Realism demands no less. To me, there are six key problems that this country needs to confront—each of which I will look at in a separate chapter.

Canada's Peacekeeping Mythology The United Nations' blue beret is a hallowed icon in Canada, and peacekeeping is something that Canadians believe is their creation and their basic military policy, something that our soldiers do better than anyone else. But was this belief ever true, or is it a myth? Is it true today? Even more important, how has peacekeeping distorted our defence policy and our national interests?

The National Interests Just what are those national interests to which Canadians and their leaders should be devoting their full attention? Are they different from Canadian values and, if so, what should be shaping our policy, interests, or values?

Dealing with the United States What about our superpower neighbour with its huge economy, powerful military, and sense of mission, the neighbour on whom we unquestionably depend for our prosperity and security? Anti-Americanism is at or near a historic peak in Canada, so powerful and venomous today that it hurts our efforts to achieve our national goals. Can Canada disagree with the United States and, if so, how should we differ and on what kinds of issues? How can we stop the Americans, exquisitely conscious of their own security weaknesses after September 11, from defending us—whether we like it or not?

Holding the Arctic The True North is more a part of Canada's mythos than it is of our reality; nonetheless, we have always looked on the Arctic as the national patrimony. Do we have the will to hold on to the North, where our fragile grasp on sovereignty is going to come under threat (not only from the Americans) as the ice melts and the Northwest Passage opens up?

A Pacifist Quebec Historical events, some positive, some negative, have shaped Quebec's place in the nation and our foreign and defence policies. Can we bring an increasingly pacifist

Quebec to a position where it will abandon its long-standing opposition to defence spending and to a vigorous Canadian role abroad? Even posing this question is, for many Canadians and Québécois, a shibboleth.

Multiculturalism and Foreign Policy Can we square Canada's policy of multiculturalism with the need for a coherent foreign policy and for domestic security? How do we grapple with Islamist terrorism at home and abroad? How can we make Canadians of immigrants from every part of the world and from different systems and traditions? To ask such questions touches on a sensitive nerve that will likely invite groundless charges of racism. But the questions are important, and they must be raised and discussed.

Two Scenarios, and the Foreign and Defence Policies We Need I begin and end this book with two scenarios, each one difficult and costly, but the second more hopeful—if we prepare properly. Every dollar spent on the military and on security serves two purposes: it helps protect Canadians at home against both terrorism and natural disasters, and it lets Canada play a role abroad. We need to be prepared for the worst that domestic and foreign nihilists and Mother Nature can throw at us. What capabilities do the Canadian Forces require to handle disasters at home and conflicts abroad in a manner that can save Canadian lives? What are the foreign and defence policies we need to deal with the new world of the twenty-first century and to provide security for our people and our land? Where can we find the will to act?

I don't have all the answers to these key questions here—I wish I did—but I have no doubt that they are the right areas to examine. If we can consider how best to deal with these problems, Canada might survive to greet the dawn of the twenty-second century as a great nation, one that continues to provide a good life for its citizens and plays a useful, important role in the world.

Canada is a greatly favoured land, but we live in a world where nations plot and connive and where the excesses of fundamentalist religions and vengeful ethnicities grow more dangerous every day. We want our nation to be a good international citizen, but it can't if we have no resources to employ abroad. We all want Canada to matter and to prosper, but unless Canadians can come to grips with modern realities, it won't. We want Canada to survive, but it won't if our wilful blindness continues. It is time to put our nation's interests first.

* * *

I owe much to many friends and colleagues for their assistance and for the discussions that have helped to form my ideas. Let me thank David Bercuson, Doug Bland, Michael Bliss, Rich Gimblett, Norman Hillmer, William Kaplan, Patrick Luciani, Alain Pellerin, Colin Robertson, Roger Sarty, Denis Stairs, and the knowledgeable contributors to the discussion pages of the Council for Canadian Security in the 21st Century (www.ccs21.org), especially Col. Gary Rice and Paul Cook. There are others I cannot acknowledge because of the positions they hold. None of them should be blamed for what follows.

I am grateful to three additional friends of long standing: Linda McKnight, my perspicacious literary agent; Phyllis Bruce, the best of publishers; and Rosemary Shipton, Canada's finest editor.

JLG

November 11, 2006

[1]

The Immediate Future: A Bleak Scenario

Tuesday, February 12, 2008 It was 7:32 in the morning when the first quake rippled through Vancouver, a city just getting itself together to go to work. It was raining hard, and the thunderstorms were almost certainly loud enough for only a few to notice the tremor. The two über-blonde hosts of the city's most popular morning television show saw their coffee jiggle, joked briefly of gremlins in the cup, and carried on discussing the city's newest high-end restaurant on Robson Street. The Pacific Geoscience Centre, phoned by one of the show's producers, said the tremor was only 3.7 on the Richter scale, nothing serious, just enough to rattle plates.

But eighteen minutes later an earthquake measuring 5.2 shook the city, knocking pictures off walls, swaying the Lions Gate Bridge, and rocking the freighters in English Bay along with the pleasure craft tied up in the city's many marinas. There were a few cracks on Pender Street's pavement where, a few minutes before, the surface had been smooth. Mothers looked at their children across the breakfast table and wondered if they should drive them to school or take them down to the basement to huddle in a corner. The morning show hosts seemed more than slightly rattled, the Geoscience Centre didn't answer the telephone, and the picture jumped on tens of thousands of TV sets. Even so, the city was used to such events. Those driving across the bridge from North Vancouver fretted that the wet, swaying roadway might delay their slow commute even more than usual.

They had no reason to worry about being late for work—everyone in the city was going to be. At 8:08 a.m. the long-feared "big one" hit Vancouver. An 8.9 quake roared through the area, the noise sounding like the passing of a freight train. The great bridge across the Lions Gate fell into the water, taking hundreds of cars and thousands of people with it. Buildings in the business core, mainly the older ones, shuddered and rocked as their electric power went down and water and gas lines burst. Fires began to spread through the basements and up to the higher floors. Cheaply constructed bungalows and condominiums fell apart, and several roads buckled. A great crevice opened up on Cambie Street. A few cars and drivers fell into the pit almost unnoticed as everyone around scrambled for safety, trying desperately to stay upright on what had suddenly become a shifting sidewalk. Buildings constructed on old mudflats or landfill almost disappeared as the land quickly liquefied to the consistency of thick soup, and, in the space of seconds, Vancouver's airport became completely unusable. The CBC, CTV, Global, and every single one of the private television channels went off the air, and almost all the radio stations became silent as the electric power supplying the region was cut. Only a few with generators stayed on the air. Computers crashed, bank machines stalled, and almost all telephone service disappeared. Then an avalanche roared down Grouse Mountain in North Vancouver, a huge mass of rock smashing everything before it, cutting roadways and Highway 99, and rolling over houses.

The Mayor of Vancouver was at home when the quake hit, but officials did not know for eight hours that he and his wife had died when their condo crumbled in the great shock. The Chief of Police was on his way to headquarters when the Lions Gate Bridge collapsed under him. His deputy tried to reach him, then stepped forward and attempted to take control of the growing chaos. Most of his force, except for the late-night and morning shifts that were in the midst of the usual handover, were scattered throughout the city and its suburbs. No one had any idea of the casualties, but as the fires took hold and as panic spread, the police, the fire departments, and the few still-functioning hospitals knew there would be more than they could handle. Many of the emergency personnel deserted their posts, desperate to find out what had happened to their families. Astonishingly, looters were already out on the streets, some young men and women pushing supermarket carts full of clothes, computers, watches, and jewellery through the downtown area. One journalist from the *Province* managed to get out of the ruins of his office at 9:20, and he saw that some of the supermarket shelves in at least one Safeway were already bare. How long would it take to get food and potable water to the city? Where were the police and the military?

What no one yet fully realized was that the quake had hit more than the Vancouver area. The Juan de Fuca Plate, stretching all the way from the Queen Charlotte Islands to California, had rubbed together with the North American Plate, and the subduction earthquake that resulted had also wreaked havoc through Washington and Oregon. Portland and Seattle, along with Vancouver, were the hardest-hit major population centres. Although all seaside cities were spared a tsunami, the coast lowered itself by more than a metre and, in some places near Seattle, the land slid as much as 6 metres seaward. The earthquake had almost completely destroyed harbour facilities from Portland through Washington to 20 kilometres north of Vancouver. And now, according to a light plane that was flying from Seattle to Abbotsford, BC, Mount St. Helen's had started to smoke again. The quake, it appeared, had activated the old, shattered volcano.

The first word of the earthquake reached Ottawa about 11:15 EST. The Government Operations Centre run by Public Safety and Emergency Preparedness Canada received the initial report; the duty officer notified his superiors and began calling in representatives of all the departments concerned. Bureaucrats quickly began putting together lists of the resources their departments had available near Vancouver, most of them assuming, rightly, that their assets in the areas directly affected would not be immediately—if ever—available. Speechwriters in the Prime Minister's Office began drafting a brief and calming statement for the country's leader to deliver.

At National Defence Headquarters, the Minister was away visiting troops in Afghanistan, where the contingent was right in the middle of its six months' rotation. Almost five thousand of the nation's best soldiers and airmen, not to mention a large part of the Canadian Forces' equipment, were either too far away to be of use in the domestic crisis or so committed that they could not readily be employed at home. In the Minister's absence, the Deputy Minister asked the Chief of the Defence Staff to provide a list of all the Canadian Forces' military assets in British Columbia. The Chief's reply came quickly: there wasn't much. The navy's Pacific Fleet headquarters in Victoria fortuitously had survived almost unscathed, but most of the ships were at sea in the Persian Gulf or on an exercise with friendly navies off Australia. The only ships available for use were four Kingston-class maritime coastal defence vessels and two frigates, a few ancient Sea King helicopters at Pat Bay, and perhaps 2,000 sailors. The ratings were quickly put on standby, but it soon became clear that the key problem was to find a way to get them ashore in large numbers, given that most of the piers in or near Vancouver had been completely or partially destroyed. None of the navy's ships could put sailors or equipment ashore in large numbers without a pier. Could civilian helicopters be used to ferry sailors to the mainland? How many were there and where? How many could still fly?

The army, similarly, had done its bleak calculations. There were about 2,000 partly trained reservists in the Greater Vancouver Area, but armouries downtown appeared to be wrecked, and the reservists were presumed to be trying desperately to save themselves and their families. There were no regular force army units in British Columbia at all because efforts to persuade the government to reopen the Army Engineers training base at Chilliwack had failed. The nearest army units were in Edmonton, across the Rockies, and a hard winter and heavy snowfalls had already made the Trans-Canada Highway susceptible to avalanches. The air force had a few patrol aircraft in British Columbia, but most of the service's transport aircraft, the one new C-17 and the twenty-eight remaining and very old Hercules C-130s, were flying in support of the troops in Afghanistan. Only eight operable Hercs were in Canada at their base at Trenton, Ontario. The troops in Edmonton and the Hercs at Trenton received orders by 2 p.m. local time to be ready to move as soon as practicable; the first task was to move the Disaster Assistance Response Team, with its hospital and water purification team, into British Columbia, a job that would tie up most of the available Hercs for at least three days. All the army's heavy trucks were more than twenty years old, clunkers held together with prayers and baling wire, and the mechanics at Canadian Forces Base Edmonton had doubts that most of them could make it to the coast.

The Prime Minister received his first detailed briefing at about the same time as the military went on standby. The word from British Columbia was horrifying. Gangs of youths were looting and setting fires, and these blazes, as well as those started by the quake, had already swept through large parts of Vancouver. The breaks in water mains and the disruption to the fire department's crews made controlling the flames impossible. Hundreds of people had been confirmed dead, but there were certainly many thousands more. Very few reports had yet reached Ottawa from smaller cities and towns where there was considerable damage, and the provincial government in Victoria so far had done little but call for help from Ottawa. After hearing this tale of destruction and the lack of resources, the Prime Minister excused himself from the meeting to call his friend, the President of the United States.

When he returned, his face was ashen. "I asked him for some

C-17s to lift our heavy equipment into Abbotsford," he said, referring to the nearest airport able to take the huge air transports. "He said his military was over-deployed as it was, supplying troops in Iraq, Afghanistan, and Central Asia. Every aircraft he had left was going to the relief of Oregon and Washington state." The Prime Minister paused. "The President said he was sympathetic to Canada's plight, but he had his own problems." Maybe the Forces ought to have bought heavy airlift earlier, he added.

Were any of the big Ukrainian or Russian air transports available for charter? one official asked. The Vice-Chief of the Defence Staff replied that this lead had already been tried, but the situation in Kyrgyzstan and the civil war in the Philippines had absorbed every single one of the aircraft until at least the end of February. "Without the Americans, without our own lift, without the charters," the Prime Minister asked, "how can we get heavy equipment and large quantities of relief supplies to the West Coast?" "There's only one way, sir. The railroads." "How long will that take?" The answer was stark: one week at the minimum, though some supplies could be dropped by parachute to cut-off areas—if the Hercs could be made available. The Prime Minister, a man with a hair-trigger temper and a penchant for cursing that the public never saw, pounded the table and shouted, "Who in Christ's name got us into this fucking mess?"

If only this tragedy had been Canada's sole crisis. While Ottawa struggled to cope with the BC disaster, two small Islamist terrorist cells in Montreal and Toronto decided to seize the opportunity to strike. They were horrified at what they saw as the godless immorality of Canada—gay marriage, public nudity, and pornography—and furious at Canada's participation in the Afghan War and its friendship with the "Great Satan" to the south. Communicating by e-mail, chatrooms, and cellphones, and going undetected by police anti-terrorist squads, they agreed to launch their attacks in the morning rush hours on Friday, February 15. The three-day delay after the earthquake, they calculated, would catch Ottawa on the hop, all resources en route west. They were correct: Canadian Forces planners had been telling the government for years that the military was completely incapable of responding to two major incidents at the same time. "If something terrible happens here at home," John Fraser, a former Conservative Cabinet Minister and long-time supporter of the military, said in 2004, "and we don't have the troops, after pretending that we do, then look out." Canada was about to find out what Fraser had meant.

The Montreal group, made up of six Algerian immigrants and two Muslim converts, one an anglophone and one an allophone, had readily purchased a truckload of sulphur, potassium chlorate, gasoline, and TNT that, armed with easily secured industrial detonators and set off with a cheap alarm clock, could make a huge explosion. Fortunately, the idea of putting ball bearings or metal scrap into the truck to create a storm of shrapnel did not occur to anyone. They planned their bomb to go off at 8:30 a.m. on the east side of Dorchester Square. The Toronto group, all but one the Canadian-born sons of Pakistani immigrants, had somehow secured several vials of anthrax spores. Their plan was to release the spores with a tiny bomb timed to explode at 8:45 a.m. and to spread the germs among subway riders at the crowded Yonge and Bloor station, the busiest point on the transit system, where major east-west and north-south lines met. Many of the passengers that morning were emergency-room physicians attending an international conference at the city's Convention Centre. Everyone who breathed in the germs would die or, at a minimum, become very sick.

The Montreal bomb made a huge bang, a great cloud of smoke, and shook several buildings. By chance, a large and heavily loaded mover's van passed by at just the right moment, absorbed much of the blast, and saved hundreds from death. Astonishingly, although many people were injured, some seriously, no one was killed except the driver—an Islamist convert desperate to achieve martyrdom—but there was near-panic in the downtown core. The Québécois had not really believed that Muslim terrorism was a threat to them, and the reaction to the explosion was sharp. It did not take long before mobs were roughing up anyone who appeared to be of Middle East origin, and women in burkas were punched and kicked. Rioting ran rampant until a very cold night put all outdoor activities, even the burning of Middle Eastern restaurants, on hold.

The Toronto terror attack was much more successful in inflicting casualties and spreading chaos. At least 3,000 people had been infected, the hospitals were trying to cope with ailing workers and doctors (who turned out to be difficult patients), and the entire subway system had been closed until it could be decontaminated. The Canadian Forces in January 2006 had launched a $300-million program to prepare for nuclear, bacteriological, and chemical attacks, but none of the sensors, robotic vehicles, or medical protective shelters had yet been delivered to the Joint Nuclear, Biological and Chemical Defence Company. In any case, the soldiers and their equipment were hundreds of miles away, and they did not make it to Toronto until the next afternoon. By then, the city's first responders were completely overwhelmed, business in the country's largest city had almost ceased, and, without the subway, the roads were in gridlock. Here, too, there were riots, and attacks on innocent Muslims soon spread to other cities in the province, leading the Premier and civic officials to call vainly for calm.

The troubles were not yet over. The terrorists had calculated their timing brilliantly. The government had commandeered Air Canada's and Westjet's passenger aircraft, and troops from Canadian Forces Bases Petawawa and Valcartier were en route to Abbotsford by Thursday, their task being to perform rescue work and restore order in Vancouver. Almost no trained regular army units were left in central Canada to help patrol the streets of Toronto and Montreal, and the bloody rioting continued sporadically over the weekend until military reservists, RCMP constables, and large numbers of Sûreté du Québec and Ontario Provincial Police officers could be mobilized and brought into the cities from outlying districts. Even so, forty-eight people were dead in Montreal, and sixty-three in Toronto, Mississauga, and Kitchener. Most of those killed were Muslims; so far as anyone knew, none were terrorists.

Now the Americans got into the act. The United States' attention ought to have been focused on the huge disasters in Portland and Seattle, but there were still enough Senators and Congressmen in Washington, DC, to charge that the Canadian terror attacks were the product of Canada's lax immigration and refugee policies and its "lousy security services," or so the Senator from New York, gearing up for her run at the presidency, described them. Demands that the border be closed, that army or National Guard patrols be mounted on the Canadian frontier, reached a crescendo. Some even renewed their calls for a fence to be built, similar to that along parts of the Mexican border. The President might have been friendly with the Prime Minister, but his advisers urged him to calm American opinion by shutting the border until further notice. He acquiesced. There would be no fence, at least not yet, but trade and tourism ceased. Factories in Canada running on a "just in time" basis suddenly found that they could not get the parts they needed. Canadian exporters trying to ship autos, manufactured goods, cattle, and foodstuffs south could not get anything into the United States. The tourist industry, already hard hit by the possibility of stringent new U.S. passport regulations, collapsed completely. Organizers cancelled two big conventions in Montreal at the last moment, and Toronto, which had never fully recovered from the effects of the SARS outbreak several years before, hunkered down and prepared for the worst. The Canadian economy, already hammered by the earthquake and the terror attacks, reeled. The Toronto Stock Exchange suffered its worst one-week decline in history, and business losses were in the tens of billions of dollars.

The government faced a withering storm of criticism as a result of both crises. Why were there not more military resources in British Columbia? people asked querulously. Why didn't the air force have the transport aircraft it needed? Just who was responsible for disaster planning, and when would he be fired? Others wondered what had gone wrong again with Canadian security and intelligence. Surely someone or some agency must have failed for two such terror attacks to succeed. And, after excoriating Ottawa, Quebec City, and Montreal

City Hall for their singular and collective failings, Montreal's isolationist and nationalist newspaper *Le Devoir* plaintively asked one day after the Dorchester Square explosion, "Why us? This isn't our war."

So who put Canada into this war against nature and against terror for which it was so obviously ill-prepared? The Prime Minister's apoplectic frustration was understandable. His government had worked to beef up the armed forces and security services with new equipment and more personnel, and it had tried to tighten the screening of immigrants and refugees. But new equipment took years to be contracted, acquired, and put into service, and policy changes took time to come into effect. A generation of inattention to Canada's defence and security needs could not be remedied in a few years.

Who put Canada into this mess? Canadians' governments had done the job, and so, too, had those Canadians who elected them. Whether we liked it or not, the Western world was at war with terrorism and, as always, with nature. Whose war was it? It was Canada's war.

[2]

The Harmful Idealization of Peacekeeping

In February 2006 the Canadian Forces took over the leadership of a coalition force based in Kandahar, Afghanistan. With their Provincial Reconstruction Team, which was to work on development projects, as well as a substantial combat capability, the soldiers' task was to root out Taliban and al-Qaeda irregulars and to give the elected Afghan government of Hamid Karzai a better chance of extending its hold across the nation. The Afghan people appeared to want this outcome too, according to opinion polls taken just two months before. Paul Martin's Liberal government had committed 2,300 troops to Kandahar in early 2005, and, soon after it took power in February 2006, Stephen Harper's Conservative government had the House of Commons endorse and extend the commitment to 2009. The Canadian Forces increased the contingent's strength towards 2,500 the following September, after the Taliban stiffened its resistance and altered its tactics.

The deployment, authorized by both the United Nations Security Council and the North Atlantic Treaty Organization, had stirred little discussion in Canada at the time it was made,* perhaps because the Martin government unaccountably felt no need to take this combat deployment to Parliament. By the spring and summer of 2006, casualties abroad had begun to mount and to receive front-page coverage, and opposition at home grew stronger. Polling suggested that the country was sharply divided, highly sensitive to casualties, and confused about Canada's goals. A Decima Research opinion poll in April revealed that 45 percent of respondents saw the Afghan deployment as a good idea, while 46 percent thought it a bad one. When asked if the troops should return home after the present one-year term of the mission, 43 percent agreed. A Strategic Counsel poll in May reported 54 percent against Canadian involvement in Afghanistan, compared to 41 percent in mid-March, with 70 percent of those in Quebec opposed. A poll in Atlantic Canada in June stated that 58 percent opposed the extension of the mission until 2009, yet, in contrary fashion, 61 percent agreed that the Canadian Forces were performing a vital mission in Afghanistan. The Innovative Research Group in June 2006 found that 59 percent of those asked supported the deployment of Canadian troops in Afghanistan (the same company's poll, taken on October 26 and 27, 2006, found a 5 percent drop in support), while Strategic Counsel in July

*A Dutch newspaper called me at the time in late 2005 when Holland was agonizing in its Parliament and media about its commitment to Afghanistan. Why, the reporter wondered, was Canada not discussing the same question, especially as an election was under way? The only answer I could provide was that Canadians seemed to pay no attention to their military.

reported intensifying opposition, with 41 percent wanting the troops brought home immediately.

Of course, it was all how pollsters spun their results—those same Strategic Counsel numbers had 21 percent supporting the retention of troops in Afghanistan "as long as it takes," with 34 percent favouring the two-year commitment. That support was higher than in the same organization's poll in May. Still, there could be no doubt that Canadians were confused and searching for direction. Strikingly, the casualties at the time of the polls were relatively light by either war or counter-insurgency standards: thirty-eight dead since the beginning of the Kandahar deployment in February 2006 and some 160 wounded in action or injured, mainly from improvised explosive devices (IEDs), suicide bombings, or in road accidents, some very seriously.* There were also an undisclosed number of post-traumatic stress casualties. What was obvious, however, was that unfavourable poll numbers tended to rise in tandem with casualties. When seven Canadian soldiers died in one week in August 2006, support for Canadian participation in most opinion polls plummeted. The Strategic Counsel reported in mid-October 2006 that although Canadians believed the decision to send troops to Afghanistan had been right (79 percent), 55 percent now thought that the price in casualties was too high to continue paying out.†

*The relationship of casualties and opinion was clear. In the beginning of August 2006, five soldiers were killed and a dozen wounded in one week. A self-selected *Globe and Mail* poll on August 7 saw 68 percent of 61,690 respondents indicating that they did not support the Canadian presence in Afghanistan.

†Contrarily, a CBC-Environics poll, released on November 9, 2006, said 56 percent did not believe the casualties constituted a good reason to leave Afghanistan. On the other hand, most wanted to withdraw before 2009.

As might be expected with Canadian troops in action, the number of columns and letters to the editor in virtually all Canadian newspapers began to expand. Some defended the mission, but others blasted the government for the deployment. What is interesting were the terms used by opponents of the Afghan mission in letters, columns, and media interviews. "We have strayed from our traditional role as peacekeepers," said one letter writer in the *Toronto Star*. Another correspondent from Vancouver, seemingly unaware that Canada had participated in the Great War, the Second World War, Korea, the Gulf War, Kosovo, and other interventions, observed: "Our role in the world has always been one of peacekeeping. How and why did we deviate from this honourable role?" Writing in Toronto's *Now* weekly, columnist Paul Weinberg noted that Canadians were "trying to absorb the sudden historic shift in mandate introduced by stealth by the Liberals." In the fiftieth anniversary year of peacekeeping, he wrote, referring to Lester Pearson's role in creating the United Nations Emergency Force during the 1956 Suez Crisis, "our troops are knee-deep in U.S.-controlled counter-insurgency" in Afghanistan. A letter writer from Victoria expanded on that theme, arguing that the role of Canadians in Afghanistan is "to support an interventionist American foreign policy in order to create an environment safe for the unimpeded exploitation of Central Asian energy resources."

Rick Salutin, a playwright, novelist, and weekly columnist in the *Globe and Mail*, thought he saw a middle ground: Canada, he wrote in July 2006, "could step back from choosing sides" and use its "relative impartiality to help broker a deal among the widest possible grouping (including the Taliban, if they want to play)." If the deal could achieve stability, "then you could use your soldiers to enforce and guarantee the agreements." If the Taliban wanted to play? Ah, if only pigs could fly! Salutin simply and wilfully misunderstood the Taliban's purpose—which is to disrupt reconstruction efforts, destroy schools and kill female students, and return fundamentalist Islam to power.* Their aim, as Christie Blatchford of the *Globe and Mail* wrote after two reporting tours in Kandahar, is "a nihilism so naked it is stunning." Nihilism apparently is more visible on the Afghan ground than it is through Salutin's rose-coloured glasses from Toronto.

*This same attitude was also displayed as some Liberal leadership hopefuls offered their responses to the Israeli attacks on Hezbollah in Lebanon in mid-July 2006. Bob Rae argued that the Harper government has missed a chance to follow in the footsteps of Lester Pearson by playing peacemaker. "Canada should have used the last 72 hours to make the case for UN peacekeeping on the border between Lebanon and Israel, accompanied by a firm timetable for a ceasefire and disengagement," Mr. Rae said. "The issue is . . . how to police borders, how to resolve tensions." Tory-turned-Liberal Scott Brison, however, said that "the fault in the initiation of this conflict was Hezbollah's. We should avoid a knee-jerk anti-Israeli positioning on this issue." Those comments drew a blast from a former Liberal foreign minister, Lloyd Axworthy, who dismissed Brison as someone so new to the party that he "doesn't really understand what Liberal foreign policy is about." Axworthy argued that Prime Minister Harper had abandoned the traditional Canadian role of honest broker in the Middle East: "He's almost at the forefront of a very small group of nations who say whatever Israel does is right ... We're becoming part of the problem, not part of the solution." NDP leader Jack Layton also called for a neutral attitude and a peacekeeping force. But all such responses miss the point. Can you be an honest broker if no one knows you're there? Or if you lack the military resources to contribute to a resolution of the crisis? Surprisingly, both national newspapers, the *Globe and Mail* and the *National Post*, suggested, correctly, that a peacekeeping force was not the answer to the Hezbollah problem. In the end, Canada did not contribute to the expanded UN Interim Force in Lebanon.

The politicians weren't far behind in their misunderstanding. New Democratic Party leader Jack Layton, and indeed all his Members of Parliament, never failed to refer to Canada's "traditional" role as a peacekeeper when wondering why the nation was involved in Kandahar. By August 2006, deftly mixing antiwar sentiment with anti-Americanism, Layton was calling for Canada to withdraw from a combat role in Afghanistan. "Why are we blindly following the defence policy prescriptions of the Bush administration?" he asked. "That course has cost dozens of lives and billions of dollars with no end in sight. Canadians want a foreign policy rooted in fact, not fear. One that is uniquely independent, not ideologically imported. And one that leads the world into peace, not follows the U.S. into wars."*

In his wonderful film *Z*, Greek filmmaker Costa-Gavras has one of his characters remark: "Always blame the Americans.

*Layton represented his supporters faithfully. His party's youth wing called for an end to Canada's "occupation" of Afghanistan at the NDP convention in September 2006. The NDP Nanaimo-Cowichan riding association submitted the following resolution to the convention: "A combat role in Afghanistan is a no-win situation both for Canada and for the Afghani people. Its only dubious value is to curry favour with the militarist government of George W. Bush. No matter how noble our intentions, such as 'bringing democracy' or 'enabling peaceful development,' these goals cannot be achieved by violence when the 'enemy' cannot be distinguished from ordinary citizens. In such a situation, Canadian troops end up acting like terrorists, destroying communities, killing and maiming innocent people. In turn our troops become easy targets for others." When published in the media, this resolution created a firestorm of negative comment, and deservedly so. The next day, the association changed the wording of its resolution. The NDP nonetheless voted overwhelmingly for an immediate pullout. No one seemed to worry about the impact of such a policy on the Afghans, on Canada's NATO allies, or on the nation's reputation for meeting commitments.

Even when you're wrong, you're right." He might have been Jack Layton, so often does he use this tactic. Layton's usually more sensible colleague, NDP defence critic Bill Blaikie, added: "I do not think we have paid sufficient attention to the departure or the significance of the change in the role of the Canadian military that our activity in Afghanistan represents." And when the House of Commons debated the Harper government's motion to extend the Afghan commitment to 2009, many Liberal members of parliament, including all but two of the leadership candidates in Parliament seeking the succession to Paul Martin, voted against the extension of the commitment their government had made. Those who spoke out sounded exactly the same as the NDP in seeing the Kandahar deployment as a change from a historic peacekeeping role to one of combat. Just what mission these former ministers and MPs thought the Martin government had accepted in Kandahar—and they had supported—remains a mystery.*

* * *

Clearly, large numbers of Canadians had come to believe that peacekeeping—traditional, blue-beret, United Nations peacekeeping—was their métier. When I became director of the old and wholly inadequate Canadian War Museum in Ottawa on July 1, 1998, the new "peacekeeping gallery" on

*Joe Volpe was in the Martin Cabinet that sent the troops to Kandahar. In an interview with *Maclean's* in October 2006, he said: "We sent over a peacekeeping, reconstruction, humanitarian group . . . we had a specific objective, we knew the goals, and we had the exit strategy. Stephen Harper changed all of that." So powerful is the peacekeeping mythology that even those who send Canadian troops to fight appear to believe that they are acting as peacekeepers.

the third floor covered almost all our post-Korea military history. This large gallery had been installed in response to visitor surveys that proclaimed peacekeeping as the Canadian role they most wanted displayed. Peacekeeping is also portrayed on Canadian coins and bills, and the peacekeeping monument near the National Gallery in Ottawa is the only major government military memorial erected since the Second World War. NATO, in contrast, the victor in the Cold War and the alliance to which Canada had devoted perhaps 90 percent of its military effort since 1949, is scarcely mentioned—though we made sure it got its full share of space in the new War Museum in the capital.

The idea of peacekeeping had its place in the nation's values, in its sense of itself. "Canada: The World's Peacekeeper," a CBC News article that is permanently available online, trumpets. The Department of Foreign Affairs website states that "peacekeeping is an important aspect of Canada's national heritage and a reflection of our fundamental beliefs." Peacekeeping, wrote historian Desmond Morton as early as 1990, "is the great morale builder" for Canadians. "It is the only thing the public think the military are any good for. It is a distraction from the military role, but it is unfortunately the one every one out there will put as priority one." In fact, the term "peacekeeping" increasingly offends soldiers for its "associated expectations and clichéd images." Peacekeeping "suggests a passive non-invasive presence operating in a benign environment . . . The reality is somewhat different," said Major Tom Mykytiuk, who had served in Afghanistan.

But no one cares what the soldiers who carry out the government's wishes might think. A recent poll, done for the Canadian

Forces by Ekos in late winter 2004–5, found 57 percent of Canadians in favour of "traditional peacekeeping" and only 41 percent favouring "peacemaking," which would involve fighting. Predictably, Québécois (62%) and the university-educated (61%) were most supportive of blue-beret peacekeeping and more opposed to confrontational peacemaking. An Environics poll for the CBC in November 2006, conducted after Canadian troops had been fighting (and dying) in Kandahar for ten months, reported that 80 percent of the public wanted the Canadian Forces to do "peace-building" while only 16 percent favoured combat roles with Canada's allies. The terms used in the polls—peacekeeping, peacemaking, and peace-building—are different, but the thrust of public sentiment is clear enough.

"Canadians keep the peace; Americans fight wars." That clichéd Canadian myth now appears to be accepted as truth from St. John's to Quebec City and from Toronto to Vancouver. Canadians proudly cite the Nobel Peace Prize that went to Lester B. Pearson in 1956 and then to United Nations peacekeepers in 1988, and they boast that this recognition was really for Canada's soldiers. They assume that, in contrast to their superpower neighbours burdened with wars and interventions from Vietnam to Panama and from Grenada to Iraq, their nation is uniquely moral in global affairs—literally, a moral superpower. An Australian columnist was half-joking when he wrote of peace-loving, incense-burning, pain-feeling, politically correct Canada. But Stéphane Dion, the Liberal foreign affairs critic, was serious when, speaking in Parliament on May 2, 2006, he said: "It is Canada's vocation to be a good citizen in the world, dedicated to peace and justice." And in August, now running for the Liberal leadership which he would win, he declared that peacekeeping was the "mandate" of the Canadian Forces. Pollster Allan Gregg, spinning a poll that showed low support for Canada's role in Afghanistan, commented that "active military combat is just not consistent with Canadians' self-image of what we should be doing abroad. For good or ill, we continue to see ourselves as kind of the Baden-Powell [Boy Scouts] of the world community, doing good deeds, not getting killed or killing others."

Of course, all this moralizing is naive foolishness. In an online discussion in March 2006, *Globe and Mail* reporter Michael Den Tandt, just back from Afghanistan, noted that "Canadians have developed a comforting mythology over the years that says the American military are warlike and aggressive, whereas our soldiers are peacekeepers. This is nonsense." The U.S. Army in Afghanistan, he said, is doing humanitarian work just as the Canadians are. "By the same token, Canadian troops are deployed in an offensive role, not just defensive . . . That means shooting and killing. That's part of what soldiers—all soldiers, including Canada's—do." And *The Economist*, the respected British weekly, acted as a spoilsport on June 29, 2006, when it noted: "The notion that Canadians do peacekeeping has become largely a myth. Among the 68,000 troops deployed on UN peace missions around the world, fewer than 60 are Canadians." The Center for Global Development, in partnership with the journal *Foreign Policy*, ranks the twenty-one richest nations' policies each year. Canada was tenth in 2006, its standing dragged down by its weak peacekeeping performance (and its pathetic performance in foreign aid). It won't matter—the myth will always override reality in Canadians' minds.

Canada is a nation without much sense of its history, and myths inevitably flourish where the facts are not taught, or are wilfully forgotten or easily ignored. It is nonetheless surprising that events of the last half-century are so misunderstood. The nation's most famous peacekeeper, Major-General (Ret'd) Lewis MacKenzie, correctly told CBC Radio's *Cross Country Check-Up* that Canada was "never a peacekeeping nation. We aren't and we never will be. At the height of our peacekeeping reputation in the 60s, 70s, and 80s, when we had about 1,500 troops in the Golan Heights, Cyprus, etc., we had 10,000 troops as part of the NATO force armed with nuclear weapons, surface-to-surface missiles, F-104s, air-to-ground missiles, waiting for the Soviet hordes to come across the border." At the same time, Canada also had much of its air force patrolling the North against Soviet bombers and working in the North American Air (later Aerospace) Defence Command, an air-defence alliance with the United States. In other words, at a time from the 1950s to the beginning of the 1990s when Canada's military effort was devoted to winning the Cold War, how was it that almost bloodless, costless peacekeeping became Canada's "traditional" role of choice in the eyes of a large segment of the Canadian public? How did it happen that so many Canadians, in Michael Bliss's splendid formulation, came to believe that "in the struggle against Communism we alternated between sitting on the fence and on the beaches of Cuba"? What are the implications of this misreading of recent history?

* * *

Lester Pearson's role during the Suez Crisis fixed Canadian—and global—attention on the idea of interposing troops from many nations between warring armies. Before 1956, UN and other peacekeeping operations were modest efforts of limited success carried out by relatively small groups of military observers. After 1956, peacekeeping was often a large-scale operation, ordinarily and regrettably also of limited success, and carried out by infantry, armoured reconnaissance, and logistics troops, as well as air force personnel, sometimes in combat roles. The difference was marked, and much of the change had occurred because of Pearson's initiative, diplomatic skill, and assessment of the need at Suez. Later crises in the Congo, Cyprus, the Middle East, Vietnam, the Iran-Iraq borderlands, Latin America, and the Sahara built on the experience of 1956, and in every case Canadian service personnel and peacekeeping expertise played an important part. More to the point, although its primary military efforts remained devoted to the Cold War, Canada also tried to be a helpful fixer, to ready its armed forces for peacekeeping, and to spread its hard-won knowledge to other nations. The designation of a standby infantry battalion for UN duty, along with army and air force peacekeeping specialists, was one sign of Canada's interest.

For years after 1950, Canadians claimed that theirs was the only nation to be represented in every UN peacekeeping mission. Participation became the symbol of Canadian nationalism, popular because it was useful, but sanctified primarily because it was something we could do for the United Nations while the Americans, the major player in the Cold War, could not. Kashmir, Yemen, West New Guinea—the list of operations went on and on.

The record was good, no doubt about it, but Canadians forget too much. They forget, first, that peacekeeping was not cost free and that more than a hundred Canadian servicemen, including twenty-eight in Cyprus and nine when a Canadian aircraft was shot down by a Syrian surface-to-air missile in 1974, were killed in UN service. None of the deaths on peacekeeping, none of those soldiers killed in Bosnia and Croatia, in Kashmir, or on the borders between Israel and its neighbours, were even noticed by Canadians or the media. Canadians loved the idea of peacekeeping, and they wanted no reminders of its costs to interfere with the warm glow that doing good gave them.

Nor do Canadians realize that peacekeeping has not been universally hailed by the countries in which troops have been deployed. Egypt, to cite one example, ejected Canadian peacekeepers in 1967, fixing the reason for this decision in part on Prime Minister Pearson's comments on the dangerous situation in the Middle East. In fact, President Nasser had decided to force a showdown with Israel and ordered the United Nations Emergency Force out of Egypt. UN Secretary-General U Thant, not one of the world organization's greatest leaders, complied. The war that the emergency force had been organized to prevent, the Six Day War, immediately broke out.

There was some humiliation in Canada at this ejection from the theatre in which Pearson had won his Peace Prize a decade before. The Egyptians lost the war, and Nasser himself was soon out of office, but no one could have argued that UNEF was a success or, because of the results of the war triggered by its expulsion, much loved in Cairo.

The Israelis may have been a beneficiary of sorts from Nasser's pique at UNEF, but they disliked UN peacekeeping every bit as much as the Egyptians. They frequently treated peacekeepers as biased or as spies and connived to fool them, humiliate them, and sometimes even entrap them. (There have been stories that General E.L.M. Burns, the Canadian who was the first commander of UNEF, had an Israeli mistress who spied for her government.) Similarly, the Indians and Pakistanis deeply resented UN observers' efforts in Kashmir and put obstacles in their way at every opportunity. The brute truth is that nations want to fight their wars and guerrilla campaigns when and how they want, and they don't like the UN or anyone else telling them what to do.

Peculiarly, Canadians do not realize that a large number of the crises that generated peacekeeping missions were never resolved and that many of the missions go on forever. UNEF failed in 1967, eleven years after its creation. What did UNEF accomplish, in fact, other than to allow both sides to rearm while blue-helmeted troops preserved "peace"? Canada went to Cyprus in 1964 and finally pulled out, completely frustrated at the absence of progress towards a resolution of the dispute, three decades later. Some servicemen had done eight or nine tours in Cyprus, and a few reportedly had second families there, with the children almost grown. The struggle between Greek and Turkish Cypriots nonetheless continues. Similarly, the Arab-Israeli conflict is never ending, despite the number and variety of United Nations and other peacekeeping forces serving in the region. In March 2006 Canada withdrew all but four of its soldiers from the UN Disengagement Observer Force on the Golan Heights after thirty-two years of service. "Mission accomplished," said a Canadian general flown in for the stand down. But it wasn't really—not with Hamas and Hezbollah rising in strength, Israeli jets buzzing the Syrian President's home, attacking missile-firing terrorists in Gaza on an almost daily basis, and waging a full-scale war against Hezbollah in Lebanon. Moreover, the tussle between India and Pakistan over Kashmir, where Canada first deployed military observers in 1950, can flare up at any moment, and it likely will. That both sides have nuclear weapons and sponsor terrorist groups only adds to the likelihood of utter disaster. Peacekeeping was "a good thing," of course, but without peacemaking, without efforts to force all parties towards a resolution, it simply did not work at all in many cases or at least work well.

Unfortunately, the Canadian public's enthusiasm for the peacekeeping concept was based on wishful thinking. The United Nations was doing the Lord's work, Canadians believed, somehow neglecting the corruption and incompetence of the UN bureaucracy (a massive investigation of bribery in placing procurement contracts for the UN's $2-billion Department of Peacekeeping was underway in late 2006) or the way the great powers used their veto in the Security Council to block action that ran against their national interests or that benefited some other power. The United Nations' failings in peacekeeping had led to the slaughters in Rwanda and, more recently, the complete failure to act to prevent genocide in Darfur in the Sudan.*

These incidents didn't matter to Canadians. Even those who recognized the UN's structural failings still believed that because we were polite and nice, everyone loved us, and our

*In his memoirs, *Navigating a New World*, Jean Chrétien's Foreign Minister Lloyd Axworthy was harshly critical of the Canadian Forces' leadership for its reluctance to take a major part in a proposed mid-1990s peacekeeping mission in the Congo. That the CF lacked the resources to do so did not appear to matter. But when Axworthy writes about the "lavish" resources of the U.S. military, he makes the point that the aggressiveness of American policy comes from the "self-fulfilling prophecy—if you have the tools you want to use them." But if you don't have the tools, you can't use them—that, too, is a self-fulfilling prophecy.

Canadian boys could resolve the differences between warring factions anywhere and everywhere that conflict reigned.

What frequently resolved matters was force. In 1991, at the onset of the wars that ripped Yugoslavia apart, the Serbs rolled into Croatia and seized one-third of its territory. The United Nations sent peacekeeping forces into the Krajina, along the no man's land between the Serb and Croatian forces. Amid the heavy fighting, there was much ethnic cleansing, and the Canadian infantry, as part of the UN force, fought a substantial pitched battle against Croatian troops in 1993 in the Medak Pocket. Two years later, now well trained and equipped, the Croats struck back in force and simply rolled over, through, and around the UN forces until they recaptured the Krajina. The UN sat and watched, completely unable to intervene.

In other words, where there is peace, UN forces can be useful as an indication that both sides are temporarily satisfied or spent. But where there is no peace, as in the Sinai in 1967 or in Croatia in 1995, peacekeepers are useless—as the Canadian-raised, hardline American conservative Charles Krauthammer has said. They can only stand by or withdraw.

The American columnist also pointed to Bosnia in 1995, where a strategic bombing campaign, not the last by any means in the Former Yugoslavia, made a difference by relieving the siege of Sarajevo and pushing Slobodan Milosevic's regime towards a negotiated settlement. Yes, the bombing had substantial effect, but it wasn't the United Nations that conducted the aerial campaign. Instead, the North Atlantic Treaty Organization's fighter-bombers did the job. This was not peacekeeping but war—bombs delivered on target by a military alliance. Instead of sitting in the middle as the UN had done with at best marginal success, NATO took sides and bombed the Serbs towards the bargaining table. As Krauthammer put it, NATO had created "a new equilibrium—a new balance of power—because that is how peace comes about: either through hegemony or through balance of power, not the urging of blue helmets." Canadians didn't grasp this fact.

There were some curious features in the Canadian attitude to the Yugoslav situation through the 1990s. One was that there were large numbers of Canadians of Croatian and Serbian descent rooting for the old home team, raising funds, buying arms, and, when they were not fighting each other on the streets of Toronto, returning "home" to serve in politics or the military. That scenario constrained Canadian policy. The nation did commit a large contingent of UN peacekeepers (over 2,000 soldiers at its peak), but Canada uncharacteristically made very little effort to secure influence on decision-making. For domestic reasons alone, that must have seemed the preferable course.

If Canadians had tried to parse the nation's role in the Balkans, they might have been forced to confront the reality that the national ideal of multiculturalism had constrained an effective peacekeeping role—or, in this case, peace enforcement—for Canada. No government, especially not the Mulroney government that put Canada into the Former Yugoslavia, could afford to appear to be taking sides in a war in which Canadian ethnic groups were on opposite sides. That was especially so for Mulroney, whose wife, Mila, is of Serbian descent. Ignorance in this case was bliss, and the Canadian battles in Croatia in 1993 received no publicity at all in this country for years.

Canadians have never understood another key factor. Traditional peacekeeping was a role the Canadian military could play not because Canada was neutral—it never was—but because Canada was a traditional Commonwealth and Western military power, used to sending troops overseas, and with its training and equipment designed for coalition service. In the 1950s and 1960s the army was relatively strong in signallers and logistics, for example, the air force in long-range transport, and the navy in projecting force far from home. In other words, Canada's wartime experiences and its post-1950 Cold War and NATO roles had shaped the Canadian Forces and made its well-trained troops eminently suitable for peacekeeping roles.

Moreover, peacekeeping ordinarily fitted seamlessly into the Cold War era. Despite perceptions at the time and since that Canada and Canadian servicemen were impartial players, peacekeeping was almost never truly neutral. Canadians deployed to the Congo in 1960 as part of a Western strategy to contain the Soviet Union's activities in newly decolonizing Africa. Canada went to Cyprus in 1964, to cite another example, because the American President, Lyndon Johnson, begged us to do so and because Greece and Turkey were NATO allies. If these two countries had gone to war over the Mediterranean island, the whole of the alliance's southern flank would have been irreparably damaged, to the great benefit of the Soviet Union and its Warsaw Pact allies. And Canada became part of the International Control Commissions in Laos, Cambodia, and North and South Vietnam in 1954 precisely because it was a Western state, balanced by the Communist Poles and the supposedly neutral Indians in an uneasy troika trying to maintain the pretense of peace in the midst of escalating violence. The Canadians, like the Poles on the commission, did not even pretend to impartiality; the Indians did pretend but were not impartial. The present-day New Democratic Party and the Polaris Institute, funded by the Council of Canadians, may choose to see peacekeeping as an impartial and neutral military activity, but this view is simply not in accord with the facts of history.

There was yet another reason the Canadian government liked peacekeeping: it believed that using its troops at UN request could enhance Canadian influence and credibility in the international arena. By playing the role of mediator and serving as one of the main providers of troops for peacekeeping, Canada sought to increase its influence within the United Nations and in some regional security institutions. This policy worked to some extent, and Canada won favour and respect from other states, especially in Scandinavia and the Third World, where most conflicts between 1945 and 1989 occurred. Through peacekeeping, Canada found a way to distinguish itself from the United States without casting doubt on its loyalty to its main ally. In other words, the blue helmet offered some benefits to Canadian diplomacy.

But the ideal of peacekeeping could constrain other important, useful actions. This limitation became obvious when Iraq invaded Kuwait in 1991 in as clear an act of aggression as the world has witnessed since 1945. The United States mobilized a vast military coalition to drive Saddam Hussein from his conquered territories. Canada took part, though hesitantly and in a small way. It was not a peacekeeping operation, though it was authorized by the United Nations, but a throwback to the kind of collective security envisaged by the drafters of the UN Charter in 1945. Canadian public opinion was sorely divided over the war, but in the end healthy majorities supported Canada's role in it. The Liberals and the New Democrats in Parliament went through conniptions trying to oppose the war while simultaneously supporting our servicemen—and women—in the Gulf. The Mulroney government, one eye fixed on public opinion, gave the troops different and progressively more aggressive mandates several times during the struggle.

One of the predominant trends in the public discourse, acerbically characterized by Charlotte Gray in the now defunct magazine of the Canadian Institute for International Peace and Security as a mixture of "idealism, legalism, internationalism and kneejerk anti-Americanism," was that, by participating in the American-led war, Canada was destroying its hard-won credibility as a peacekeeper. There was unquestionably an element of anti-Americanism about all this, not least in the Opposition's stances in Parliament, in much of the media coverage, and in the positions taken by the various peace groups. And support for peacekeeping, because it was deemed by the public to be Canada's particular skill, became one of the main vehicles for expressing this hostility.

The critics who charged that the government had sacrificed Canada's peacekeeping role on the altar of Washington's war over Kuwait and oil were proven wrong almost at once. Within weeks of the end of the Gulf War, Canada was asked to participate—with seven hundred soldiers and the force commander—in a UN peacekeeping operation being set up in the Sahara to supervise a referendum designed to end the long war between Polisario guerrillas and Morocco. The country was also expected to participate, and did, in a UN force in Cambodia. Soon thereafter, Canada sent land-mine removal teams to work under a UN force along the Kuwait-Iraq border. So much for the idea that participation in the Kuwait war would destroy Canada's peacekeeping reputation. But what self-respecting state would decide matters of great national import by clinging to an image of itself as a blue-bereted middleman?

The point should be obvious: for too many Canadians, the ideal of peacekeeping had become a substitute for policy and thought. Some countries try to deal with problems by throwing money at them; our people and, to some substantial extent, our governments tried to deal with the world's problems by sending peacekeepers. This is not an ignoble impulse, but it is one that has to be checked with realism. Canada was right to participate with its allies in the war against Saddam Hussein in Kuwait, and those who objected to our role, whether out of misguided anti-Americanism or concern for our future as a peacekeeper, were flatly wrong. We have also been right to participate in most of the peacekeeping operations in which we have served. But, at the very least, let us retain and enhance our right to consider which peace-support operations we shall participate in, just as we have the right to consider which wars we shall fight. Governments, like individuals, are supposed to be capable of rational decision-making. And automatic responses—whether "My country right or wrong" or "Send in the Canadian peacekeepers"—are no substitutes for thought.

But there was still more in the Canadian misunderstanding of peacekeeping. It was never something Canada did on its own. When the Canadian Army and other national contingents deployed to Suez in 1956, for example, American stockpiles of equipment were needed for the United Nations Emergency Force to function. Similarly, when the Canadian Forces sent army signallers to the Iran-Iraq borders after the end of Saddam Hussein's bloody war against the Iranian mullahs in 1988, American aircraft had to be employed to carry their heavy equipment, and the United States provided the signals equipment that could operate effectively in mountainous terrain, where Canadian wireless sets could not. In other words, even when Canada tried to take a lead role, Uncle Sam frequently had to play his part to make the blue-helmet idea work. Canadians simply did not understand their limits.

Finally, crucially, the Canadian public did not grasp that, with the end of the Cold War, peacekeeping had changed. As noted before, the unleashing of ethnic nationalism in Yugoslavia, for example, tore that country apart and spawned a series of peace-enforcement missions in Bosnia, Serbia, Croatia, and Kosovo. In Croatia, Canadians fought battles and, during the Kosovo crisis, Canadian troops and aircraft participated in a war against Milosevic's regime in Belgrade. The present Afghan War against the Taliban and al-Qaeda, also authorized by the UN Security Council, is far closer in the way it is being waged to post-1991 "peacekeeping" than it is to any UN missions mounted while the Cold War went on. The world has changed, and "peacekeeping" now requires a full suite of weaponry and well-trained troops. The United Nations may have dropped out of most of the tough peacekeeping missions, but that is only because it could not mount the well-armed coalitions needed for present-day peace enforcement. Just as in Bosnia and now in Afghanistan, NATO or coalitions of the willing have to step in when the United Nations cannot do the job.

* * *

If this bleak picture is the reality, and it is, why, then, is peacekeeping still such a cherished part of the Canadian national mythos? There are many reasons, such as the misplaced national joy that Canada can do something that the Americans can't, and the idea that a multicultural Canada—one, moreover, with a pacifist Quebec uneasily in its bosom—ought not to engage in military actions that might further fray the bonds of unity. There is also Canadians' unabated and continuing affection for the United Nations, an attitude that continues despite the organization's inability to reform itself, its rampant corruption, and its failings in keeping the peace or in uniting to punish aggressors and genocidal dictators. But the major reason Canadians and their governments mythologize peacekeeping is simple and clear: the costs of mounting and maintaining modern defence forces are such that peacekeeping seems the cheapest way to operate.

The Liberals under Jean Chrétien, adopting and expanding the policy followed by the Trudeau and the Mulroney governments, allowed the Canadian Forces to decay to the point where Paul Martin's successor government had to act—sometime. The Martin administration's 2005 promises of more money for defence were scheduled to take effect in 2009–10, well past the life of that government, which in fact disappeared in electoral defeat in January 2006. The new Conservative government of Stephen Harper also pledged to rebuild the Canadian Forces, and in June that year announced plans to spend an astonishing $17.1 billion on new helicopters, trucks, Joint Support Ships, and long- and medium-range transport aircraft. The Tories' detailed defence plans, thus far, remain substantially unformed beyond a commitment to a "Canada First" strategy that, frankly, can mean almost anything. Moreover, with a small minority government, the Conservative grasp on power is uncertain at best. With new Liberal leader Stéphane Dion in favour of a "professional review" of Canada's Afghanistan mission, with the New Democratic Party and the Bloc Québécois both irredeemably hostile to any military involvement with the United States or any roles other than the most benign forms of UN peacekeeping, absolutely nothing is certain for the future state or roles of the Canadian Forces. The sole exception is peacekeeping, our "traditional peacekeeping," the one military role that is both popular with Canadians and viewed as the embodiment of Canadian values—different values, of course, from the war-making proclivities of the United States.

Why? Because peacekeeping is "good," Canadians say, and peacekeeping seems relatively inexpensive. The cost of defence has been, is, and will remain a determinant of Canadian defence policy. Although Canada in some years in the 1950s spent more than 7 percent of its gross domestic product on defence, the numbers more recently have dwindled to just above 1 percent. The strength of the Canadian Forces, 120,000 at the beginning of the 1960s, is now at a nominal 62,000, but in reality there are only 53,000 effectives—men and women trained and available for service. The reserves—the part-time soldiers, sailors, and airmen and women—as well as the Canadian Rangers who operate in the North, total some 25,000 in various stages of training. They include students earning money in the summer as well as highly trained and ready-to-deploy helicopter pilots. The Conservative government has promised to add 13,000 to the regular forces and 10,000 to the reserves, but, even in the best of circumstances, that is a long-term project. And, with a low rate of unemployment nationally, a badly broken recruiting system, and the Canadian

Forces expecting some 15,000 of its present members to retire or resign in the next few years, these are not the best of circumstances in which to increase the size of the Canadian Forces.

If increasing the personnel strength of the services is problematic, so too is raising the defence budget to well above $20 billion from its present level of $14 billion. Canada's defence spending (measured as a percentage of gross domestic product) is well below that of other G-8 countries and at the bottom level of NATO members, with only Luxembourg and Iceland doing less. In per capita spending, Canada puts up $343 for each man, woman, and child to defend Canadian national interests at home and abroad.* Great Britain spends $903; Australia, $648; and the Netherlands, $658. Keeping up with the Joneses' defence spending can be costly. The high cost of a wide-spectrum defence force has made peacekeeping very attractive to cost-conscious governments pressed to deal with other urgent priorities such as a national child-care program and the voracious maws of medicare and higher education. I am in favour of all such provisions, but I agree with the title of the June 2006 report of the Senate's Standing Committee on National Security and Defence: "The Government's No.1 Job: Securing the Military Options It Needs to Protect Canadians."

The senators were correct. Without adequate defence, everything else can be lost.† But a strong defence is expensive, and Canadians have fallen in love with peacekeeping because it is

*If the Canadian government carries out its announced plans, per capita defence spending will come closer to that of Australia and the Netherlands by 2011.

†Canadians appear to agree with this statement. An Innovative Research Group poll in June 2006 found 62 percent agreeing that "without national security, all other individual rights become theoretical."

virtuous and, above all, as General Lewis MacKenzie put it, peacekeeping is "deemed to be cheap, because you don't need all the equipment" to fight a war. The Canadian Forces' equipment, much of it obsolete, requires replacement with modern kit at very high prices. Successive governments, Liberal and Conservative, he said sourly, "have impressed upon the Canadian people [that] we've got this peacekeeping reputation to spread around the world. We will solve all these problems by insightful thoughts."

Simply put, the relative inexpensiveness of peacekeeping looked good to governments. No wonder government agencies such as the CBC and the Department of Foreign Affairs constantly tout Canada's virtues as the world's pre-eminent peacekeeper. It seemed to be the cheapest way of paying for defence and making Canadians feel good about themselves. The great peacekeeping myth let Canadian governments pretend to have a military while they use the dollars saved for other purposes. "The logic of a diminished Canadian military is easy to grasp," the U.S. Army's Colonel Joseph Nunez wrote. "Internationally, Canada enjoys the security umbrella afforded by the United States. Thus, it acts as a free rider and can fund its defense on the cheap. Monies not devoted to defense are used to pay for domestic programs." All that is squandered is real sovereignty and influence. As Nunez said bluntly but dispassionately, "Canada used to take pride for being able to 'punch above its weight.' Now it punches below its weight."

As the Liberals knew and the Harper government has discovered, the modern equipment needed to get Canada back into its appropriate weight class as a G-8 nation will cost billions. If Canada today wants to deploy even lightly armed peacekeepers abroad, it needs ships, aircraft, trucks, helicopters, and all the traditional kit and caboodle to do so. Even the most benign blue-beret peacekeeping is not cheap any longer; vigorous peacemaking is much more expensive and costly in lives.

But peacekeeping alone could never be the answer for Canada in the dangerous world of the twenty-first century. Like all countries, Canada faces threats, both terrorist and existential, and no one who predicted an end to major wars has ever been proven right. Nations still need armies and they will into the future, so long as they have national interests to protect.

Yes, Canada should support the United Nations and do peacekeeping when it can—and, yes, this peacekeeping should include efforts with others to stop the slaughters in the Congo, Lebanon, and Darfur. That being said, it is important to note that none of these crises comes close to being "traditional peacekeeping," whatever those who call for Canadian participation might claim. The Congo and Darfur conflicts are akin to civil wars or jihads, with mass slaughters of civilians by well-armed but ill-disciplined irregular troops, and both might produce far more casualties to Canadian soldiers deployed there than the Afghan War. The Lebanese tragedy featured a conflict between Israel, a regional military superpower, and Hezbollah, a large, well-armed terrorist organization deeply entrenched, literally and figuratively, in south Lebanon and supplied with armaments by Iran and Syria. Moreover, neither Darfur nor the Congo are territories with the infrastructure a Western army needs to operate—unlike Afghanistan, where first the Soviet and then the American military built the airfields, hospitals, and water plants and provided other basic needs. There is no way to get Canadian troops and equipment into these hell-holes easily and, even more important, no way to get the troops out quickly in an emergency. Still, whenever it is able, Canada should do what it can in UN peace operations and, when it serves Canada's interests to do so, in peace-support operations with NATO or with ad hoc coalitions. That national-interest test is very important, and Canadian governments should apply it to every suggestion that Canada dispatch its men and women abroad. I will say much more about national interests in the next chapter.

With the forces and equipment on hand today, Canada's ability to act abroad is severely limited. As the Chief of the Defence Staff, General Rick Hillier, told a parliamentary committee in the autumn of 2006, "We do not have the resources to put in every single spot around the world that needs our help desperately. We are now at the extreme limits of what we can contribute anywhere . . . and obviously Canada is not the sole source to provide that help. Maybe some of those other countries have to step up to those other places." In an article written in 2003, Michael Ignatieff (then at Harvard University) said: "You can't do any development, you can't get any order in these [failed] societies unless you have combat power on the ground. This is the new reality we are in and this is the reality we have to do something in Canada to fix, and you can't fix it by spending 1.1 percent of GDP on national defence . . . We've got to spend more," he went on, "if we want to have any influence in Washington, if we want to have any legitimacy as a multilateralist, if we want to keep any of the promises that we are making to ourselves in the mirror and to people overseas."

Our promises in the mirror ought to have become obvious in July 2006. During the fighting in Lebanon, the politicians, public, and media demanded that Canada evacuate the 50,000 Canadian citizens living in or visiting that sad nation. Why couldn't Canada use helicopters, they asked, to move people to aircraft carriers offshore as the French and Americans were doing? It did not occur to those caught in the region, perhaps because many of them had not been in Canada in decades, that Canada had no carriers and few helicopters, and that there was almost no way to get the choppers to the Middle East. The government did its best by chartering ships, but Liberal critics, forgetting how their government had slashed the Canadian Forces' budgets, attacked the slowness of the response. No one ever seems to expect that politicians should be either fair or sensible.

The military's present personnel situation is critical. Whether the army's Afghan commitment can be sustained beyond two years, for example, is not certain; it will probably be impossible if the Canadian Forces are called on to dispatch a task force of 1,000 to 1,500 soldiers anywhere else, including Darfur, the Congo, and the Israeli-Lebanon border, where Canadians (and others) in the summer of 2006 demanded another peacekeeping force with a mandate robust enough to separate the Israelis and Hezbollah. (The UN force stationed in Lebanon turned out to be both toothless and understrength, unable and unwilling to stop Hezbollah's rearming, despite UN resolutions.) So short-staffed is the army for infantry, so limited is the availability of LAV IIIs—the army's excellent light-armoured vehicles—that it would be practically impossible to send a contingent to any such war zone or to the next area of crisis, wherever that might be. But the critics of the government, the opponents of the Afghanistan operation, simply fail to take such basic factors into account.

None of them ever talk of logistics or the availability and rotation of personnel; all appear to assume that a thousand Canadian soldiers can be deposited into the jungle or the desert and instantly function as keepers of peace. They can't. The rebuilding of the Canadian Forces promised by the Conservatives is essential if Canada is to have any capabilities to exploit in the years after 2010. Along with a national-interest calculus, the government needs to assess the Canadian Forces' capabilities carefully before it accepts requests to deploy anywhere.

The simple truth is that Canada is a small country, at best a mid-rank middle power, with limited resources. There is little it can do on its own and, with its present military strength, relatively little it can do in cooperation with its friends. Even basic peacekeeping, let alone a major peace-support operation over and above the Kandahar commitment, is beyond Canadian capacity in 2007.

But there are some things we must do, some interests to which we must attend. Above all, Canada must protect its national interests in North America and use what strength it has to act with other democratic states elsewhere in the world. We are not neutrals and, given our geographical location, our history, and our heritage, we cannot be neutral. Substantial numbers of the public argue that Canada should adopt a neutral stance—or at least one that does not favour Israel—when the Israelis fight Hezbollah in Lebanon, and perhaps we could then play "honest broker." The territory in dispute is not directly relevant to Canada, although the volatile nature of the region and the likelihood of a war in Lebanon spreading widely should concern Canadians. More directly, however, Hezbollah, a terrorist organization, and one declared as such by the Canadian government, attacked a neighbour. That conduct should concern Canadians, who, whether they like it or not, are part of the War on Terror, both as a target and as a participant. Would neutrality have been the correct position in the Hezbollah war? Likely not, and the Conservative government made clear that it stood with Israel in fighting the terrorist group that had attacked it. Stephen Harper, wrote L. Ian Macdonald in the *Montreal Gazette*, "sees no moral equivalency, none at all, between Israel and Hezbollah, between a democracy and a terrorist organization pledged to its destruction. Good for him." The Israelis acted on their assessment of their national interests; so, too, did the Harper government.

Canada has clear national interests we must protect. Canadian Forces that are well trained and equipped can fight in war and play a role in vigorous peace-support missions, protect Canadian sovereignty and contribute to the defence of the continent, and, in addition, play a part in blue-beret peacekeeping. But the reverse is not true: Canadian Forces that are devoted only to peacekeeping will not be able to do anything else and, inevitably, will be little more than a badly trained and lightly equipped gendarmerie wearing UN blue helmets and subject to the will of a wobbly multilateral consensus at the United Nations. A public fixated on neutrality and believing that Canada should field only impartial peacekeeping forces will never understand the requirements of national defence or satisfy its inchoate desire for Canada to play a meaningful role in the world. The defence of Canadian national interests will always require much more than blue berets, and the protection of our nation demands that we be committed. When he visited London on July 14, 2006, Prime Minister Harper referred to the War on Terror and said, "Canada's new national government is absolutely determined, once again, to stand shoulder to shoulder with our British allies, to stay the course and win the fight." Such words need to be said—and said again.

Nations need myths to put the story of their past into heroic form and to offer a template for use in shaping their present and future course. Some myths can be corrosive and lead to aggression and hyper-nationalism, but Canadians happily have few of those stories to bedevil them. Instead, we have great dollops of wishful thinking on which we base our present attitudes and, too frequently, our policies. These myths are dangerous to our survival today, and for our foreseeable future, because they sometimes distort our policy-making. Some hard-eyed realism, some recognition of our national interests and what we need to protect and advance them, would serve Canada and Canadians far better.

Captain Kevin Schamuhn commanded a Princess Patricia's Canadian Light Infantry platoon in Afghanistan, and he and his men saw some tough action. A Royal Military College graduate and a student of military history, the twenty-six-year-old officer told *Toronto Star* reporter Mitch Potter that he would understand if someone returned from Kandahar and declared himself a pacifist. "But if you're born in Canada and that's all you've ever known, your words mean nothing to me. Because you haven't seen the other side of the world," he continued. "You haven't seen the necessity of conflict. There are people who are fighting against peace, against stable government." Then Schamuhn said words that many Canadians find unutterable: "And Canada, whether they want to know it or not, has a very strong warrior class. I guess that is what the front-line soldiers really want Canadians to understand. We want Canadians to get on board, to realize we are out here and to allow us to do what we are prepared to do." The soldiers were prepared to fight against al-Qaeda and the Taliban, for peace, and for Canada's national interests.

In July 2006, Lieutenant-Colonel John Conrad, commanding the National Support Element of the Canadian contingent in Kandahar, phrased the issue concisely. "Canadians care about having a voice in the world, and that voice goes silent without boots on the ground," the *Globe and Mail*'s Christie Blatchford quoted him as saying. "You want a voice at the G-8, you gotta pay. I think Canada is ready for that." I hope he's right, but neither the polls nor the comments of most of the media and politicians in 2006 suggested anything except that Canada's peacekeeping myth remains intact. Derek Burney, a former Ambassador to the United States, remarked how troubling he found the "apparent unwillingness of our society to support actions intended to sustain the liberty and security we often take for granted."

The liberty and security we take for granted. It's our war and, as we shall see in the chapters that follow, we are fighting it in Afghanistan and at home. Writing the day after four Canadian soldiers were killed and ten wounded in Afghanistan, Blatchford stated emotionally that "the war is on. Canada did not declare it, but it has come to our shores as surely as it came to Manhattan's five years ago. Our soldiers are dying for it, in Afghanistan, but they are also fighting for Canadians. The least we can do—and we do, in this country, prefer to do the least—is stiffen our collective resolve, face up to the truth, and recognize that the soldiers' terrible sacrifice is in our name."

[3]

What Really Matters: Canada's National Interests

Paul Heinbecker was one of the stars of the Department of Foreign Affairs and International Trade. He had been in the diplomatic service for four decades, serving around the globe, directing the United States Division in Ottawa, and chairing the policy secretariat. He was the number two diplomat in Washington, the foreign policy adviser to Prime Minister Mulroney, Ambassador to Germany, an Assistant Deputy Minister, and, finally, after 2000, Canada's Ambassador to the United Nations. In his last post, Heinbecker tried to negotiate a way out of the war against Iraq. His is a record of achievement.

But Heinbecker sounded very much like Lloyd Axworthy, Canada's Foreign Minister from 1996 to 2000, in a speech he gave soon after he took up his post at the United Nations: "Canadians," he proclaimed, "are moved by humanitarian impulse, not by the cold-blooded or rational calculations of *realpolitik*. Principles are often more important than power to Canadians."

Now think what that means. The desire to help and the need to stand up for our principles are the key factors for Canadians and, by clear implication, their country's diplomats and foreign ministers. Not for us hard-edged calculations of *realpolitik*, the Bismarckian phrase that suggests a foreign policy based on strictly practical rather than idealistic notions and waged without any sentimental illusions.* *Realpolitik* means doing whatever is necessary to protect national interests. In other words, to Heinbecker, national interests are not important, certainly not as important as humanitarianism, principle, and, presumably, values. Heinbecker's views were very much those of the government of Canada and the Department of Foreign Affairs at the beginning of the twenty-first century and, indeed, he was one of the main creators of Canada's policy on human security.

In my opinion, the denigration of national interests, as espoused by Heinbecker, is almost wholly wrong, naive, and ultimately misguided. Of course, Canadians want their nation to help those who are suffering. Naturally, we want our leaders to be principled men and women with a conscience. But nations do not exist in a fairy-tale world where good always triumphs, where the cowboys in white hats inevitably beat up the bad guys in black hats. Nations, big and small, push and prod

*"The case for realism in our foreign policy," Allan Gotlieb wrote to Pierre Trudeau in 1967, "derives much of its urgency and strength from an appreciation of the consequences of national policies based upon immature or unreal concepts of internationalism. False internationalism leads to disillusionment, and the consequences of disillusionment are isolationism and withdrawal." Ambassador Gotlieb would likely be the first to concede that Prime Minister Trudeau did not always heed this advice, as Canadian foreign policy in those years swung erratically between the poles of aggressive nationalism and unrealistic internationalism.

their neighbours, seeking territory, trade, or influence. Leaders, powerful and unprincipled, try to rouse their populations to love or hate those in the nation next door. It's not a benevolent world out there, and the cold-blooded or rational calculations of *realpolitik* are sometimes precisely what are needed.

Heinbecker was not alone in his naive idealism. In 2003 Jean Chrétien's Foreign Minister, Bill Graham, released a paper intended to launch an online consultation on foreign policy with Canadians. The paper called flatly for a values-based policy. "Canada's foreign policy agenda must reflect the nation we are: a multicultural, bilingual society that is free, open, prosperous and democratic," it said. "The experiences of immigrants from around the world and the cultures of our Aboriginal peoples are woven into the fabric of our national identity. Respect for equality and diversity runs through the religious, racial, cultural and linguistic strands forming our community." The paper went on to urge that Canada "promote our values" abroad, such as "our long-standing advocacy of human rights, the rule of law, democracy, respect for diversity, gender equality and good governance."*

*After the Liberals lost power, Graham became Leader of the Opposition until the leadership convention in December 2006 selected a successor to Paul Martin. Nothing changed in his ability to confuse interests and values, however. After Prime Minister Harper's first visit to the White House in July 2006, Graham insisted that Canada must keep its own interests at heart at all times. Fair enough. But, he proclaimed, "a change in attitude which creates a closer, cozier relationship with the American administration has never in the long run been good for Canada." That, historically, was nonsense. Graham presumably preferred the anti-Americanism practised by the governments in which he served, and particularly by Paul Martin during the 2005–6 election. By no account had that deliberate provocation been good for Canada.

Few Canadians, if asked, would disagree with much of this preachy squishiness; indeed, most who responded online believed that Graham's list of values covered just about everything that mattered to Canada. The respondents, I suspect, would have been hard pressed to identify Canada's national interests, and they might well argue, as Paul Heinbecker did, that humanitarianism and principle were more important to Canada than national interests. I disagree completely, and this chapter will take a harder-edged look at what really matters to this nation in the twenty-first century.

* * *

Canadians instinctively believe that their nation is a moral superpower. We know that, with our 32 million people inhabiting a sprawling half-continent, we are no military superpower. We realize that our military strength, compared to that of our superpower neighbour, is puny. We even understand that we cannot match the military strength of Britain, France, Germany, or even Sweden. But that is immaterial to Canadians. What matters to us is that old cliché—our strength is as the strength of ten because our hearts are pure. We have no goals against other states, no historic grievances, no vaunted ambitions. We do not even have national interests, but only values such as tolerance, gender equity, multiculturalism, good governance, and general all-round wholesomeness. We are against big armies, against compulsory military service, against nuclear weapons, and in favour of disarmament. Canadians are the world's good guys, the nation that always does the right thing and is not afraid to tell the rest of the world, especially the United States, just what the right thing happens to be. As the beer advertisement a few years ago put it, "I am Canadian," and that's sufficient.

Naturally enough, such a nation can have no enemies. The United States might be hated and feared around the world, but not Canada. Our teenagers ensure that they put a Canadian flag on their backpacks as they travel, so no one will mistake them for Yanks. And because everyone loves us, we are not a target. Terrorists might threaten the United States, but no one wants to hurt us. The horror of September 11 could never be visited on Canada. I am Canadian, I am a peacekeeper, our citizens say, and we are the world's moral superpower with armed forces that can threaten no one. And, we add, there is no one to threaten us and, were any to try, well, the Americans would defend us. What, after all, could be better for a nation as blessed as ours?

A good dose of reality might be better. Myths are no basis for policy. Take the moral superpower argument, to start with. The Swedes, Europe's perpetual neutrals, have played the moral superpower card ever since the Great War and have a virtual patent on the phrase—there is even a book by the Swedish scholar Ann-Sofie Dahl called *Sweden: The Moral Superpower*. It's not true for the Swedes, as Dahl notes; it's even less true for Canadians, who have always had their national interests and have actively tried to advance them. We bargain toughly for trade advantages with our friends and foes; we try to achieve our goals by making the treaties and agreements we negotiate favour us; and, to be brutally frank, we use the card of moral superiority to help us get our way. Lloyd Axworthy, Chrétien's Foreign Minister, was a master at playing this role, "guilting" most of the world into directing attention to his human security agenda and almost—but not quite—dragging the United States into endorsing the anti-personnel land-mines treaty that he shepherded into international law. (Ultimately, forty-four nations did not sign on, mostly those facing military threats and including the United States, Russia, and China, though none at home in Canada seemed aware of this point.)

We have values—good values—and they matter greatly in telling Canadians who we are and who we think we are as a people. It is, however, a moot question whether we should be trying to export our values around the world, practising a kind of do-gooder Boy Scout imperialism that says, "Our values are better than yours. Take them, Saudi Arabia, or North Korea, or Iran." Those Canadians who bridle at President George W. Bush's efforts to make the Middle East democratic might at least pause to wonder how different our own values-based approach to enlighten the world has been at root. In fact, as a major paper entitled *In the National Interest: Canadian Foreign Policy in an Insecure World*, prepared by the Canadian Defence and Foreign Affairs Institute in 2003, noted, "trying to remake the world in Canada's image is a hugely ambitious project; if one were to take it seriously, it would entail more resources than Canadians have at their disposal." There was no problem, however: "The government in Ottawa devotes very little of Canada's national treasure to international affairs." As a result, the paper continued, "trying to project Canadian values abroad has turned into a largely hypocritical exercise." Canada talks a good line, but doesn't even try to spend the money to make its policies work. Our foreign aid is at 0.27 percent of gross domestic product, while the usual and accepted global target is 0.70 percent. How many Canadians understand that foreign aid is lagging? How many manage to ignore the yawning gap between governmental feel-good pronouncements and reality? Almost all, I expect.

The result of decades of preachiness from diplomats like Heinbecker and politicians like Lloyd Axworthy or Bill Graham has been the fostering of naive, moralistic mythologies. Regrettably, most Canadians genuinely believe that we are a moral superpower, setting the global standard in everything that matters. As *In the National Interest* put it, "concentrating on the projection of our values abroad has encouraged Canadians to lose sight of the central importance of interests in the responsible conduct of foreign affairs." Tilting at windmills may be pleasing to the Canadian soul, but it squanders human and fiscal resources.

The point is straightforward: we have national interests that must be protected and advanced if we are to survive as a nation-state. Canadian national interests are simple and clear. As with any nation, Canada must protect its territory, maintain its unity, and enhance its independence. It must expand its economy to improve the welfare of its people and, as a small country with global interests, it must work with others to advance democracy and freedom. Those interests have traditionally determined Canada's course, and they must continue to do so.* They deserve examination.

* * *

*The first real statement of national interests was offered by Secretary of State for External Affairs Louis St. Laurent in a speech at the University of Toronto in January 1947. He explained that Canada's foreign policy was founded on national unity, political liberty, the rule of law, the values of Christian civilization, and a willingness to accept international responsibilities.

The primary responsibility of every state, including Canada, is to protect its people and its territory. The Standing Senate Committee on National Security and Defence put it this way in its 2006 report: "The most basic role of any national government is to protect its citizens and their vital interests." A nation that cannot protect the people living in its territory is not a true nation-state. Every government is continually facing hard choices, but if a conflict arises among different interests, this obligation to protect must be the key in making the tough decisions. The Harper government appears to have grasped this responsibility instinctively with its "Canada First" defence policy: the aircraft, trucks, ships, and helicopters it is buying can be used anywhere in the world, but they can also be used at home. "Canada First" suggests that the priorities of the Conservative government are the right ones.

Second, every nation must protect its independence, its ability to make autonomous decisions that serve the interests of its people. This goal is easy to state but hard to achieve. Canada began its life as a nation-state in 1867 as a British colony, with decisions on foreign policy made for it in London. The country went to war in 1914 at the same time as Britain because, as a colony, Canada had no right to declare war on its own. A quarter-century later, Canada again went to war, though this time, after the Statute of Westminster of 1931, it had the right to have King George VI declare war on its behalf. Did anyone in Ottawa do a national-interest calculus to determine if Canada was threatened? Not really. It was enough that Britain had declared war against Germany, enough that Canada still felt strong allegiances to the King and the British Empire-Commonwealth.

We assumed that Britain would defend us if necessary, an idea that disappeared in May and June 1940 after the fall of France and Dunkirk. Britain's military weakness forced Canada to turn to the United States and, in the Ogdensburg Agreement, to create the Permanent Joint Board on Defence. Ottawa had no other possible choice, none at all, and the United States committed to defend us if we were attacked. That was the right decision for Canada and the United States in 1940. But after the war, and especially since the end of the Cold War, Canadians have not been prepared to spend much on defence in times of peace. The Americans, we still say, will defend us if we are attacked. That's likely true, but American national interests are not necessarily the same as Canadian. What happens if our interests and theirs diverge? The United States will act in its own interests, and so it should. Will Canada? Our decisions as a nation need to be calculated carefully so that they enhance, not threaten, our independence.

In considering our defences, we have to remember that Canada's independence and its sovereignty over its territory cannot be defended by anyone else. We need to provide and pay for it, with capabilities that can secure our borders and protect our people. We need to maintain, secure, and defend the territorial integrity of Canada and the safety of Canadians at home. The national interest of enhancing independence must shape our defence decisions. As Michael Ignatieff put it in a lecture in Ottawa in March 2004 (before, as Rick Mercer phrased it so neatly, he made the hard decision to immigrate to Canada to seek the Liberal leadership): "We do not want to arrive at a situation where Canadian lives are in danger, at home or abroad, and we have to be dependent on someone else's capabilities, whether diplomatic, intelligence or military, to get us out of trouble. A helping hand *from* a friend is one thing, dependency is another. A helping hand *to* a friend is one thing—and so we should provide security cooperation, border monitoring in a close and cooperative manner—but subservience is another. Negatively, we must not be dependent, and we must not be subservient. Positively, we must stand on our own two feet." That's what independence means.

The maintenance of the nation's unity is also a key interest. Going to war in 1914 and 1939 appealed to most English-speaking Canadians, but it did not move the vast majority of French Canadians into the desire to fight. Prime Ministers Sir Robert Borden and William Lyon Mackenzie King, in their own different fashions, grappled with the question of unity and tried to manage it. Historians generally agree that King, who had the benefit of learning from Borden's mistakes, did better, but in neither of the world wars did the country's founding peoples work as one. The best we can say is that Canada did not split apart from its internal tensions, but every prime minister since the end of the Second World War in 1945 has had to look hard at the state of Canadian unity. If Canada stays together, this necessity will be a brake on foreign and domestic policies into the future. If Quebec ever separates, Canada will be diminished geographically, economically, and in its standing in the world. But at the same time, Canada will still need to work to keep Atlantic Canada and Western Canada united with Ontario, and that task will likely become increasingly difficult. The need for unity, in other words, has been, is, and will remain a national interest. It goes without saying that the maintenance of a united, sovereign nation within the existing territorial boundaries must be the key national interest, and this objective requires the federal government to oppose separatism vigorously.

Canada can be independent and united only if its economy grows and its people's prosperity is enhanced. The way to achieve these goals is not always clear. In the 1950s and 1960s, Canadian governments fought hard to protect what was left of the nation's economic autonomy. The battle was waged over how much American investment the country could tolerate and, to some extent, which sectors of the economy had to be preserved (banking, for example). Rules and regulations were put in place, not always with broad public support and frequently in the face of the vituperative condemnation of substantial segments of the Canadian business community. The American government certainly resented Ottawa's efforts, and it used its policies to rein in what it believed were Ottawa's excesses. After the 1988 election on free trade, however, the issue of foreign investment all but disappeared, only to be replaced by great public and governmental concern over how free Canadian access truly was to the U.S. market. The long-running dispute over softwood lumber illustrates the new concern.

How best to interpret the national economic interest may be difficult. What is certain is that Canadians understand that theirs is a free-enterprise country. We believe in markets because we know they are better than governments at allocating capital and labour and because free markets have tended to create free peoples. But we also know that capitalism cannot be allowed to operate without check, and we accept that our political community cannot endure if it is not sustained by the public provision of medicare, social security, and some measures of equalization of revenues among the provinces.

The reality for us is that Canada's prosperity depends on our proximity to and trade with the United States. Some indeed, not least *In the National Interest*, argue that Canada has only one true interest—successfully managing the relationship with the United States. Our livelihood as a people and our security as a nation depend on getting this relationship right. The difficulty is that our independence is most at risk through our relations with our closest neighbour, best friend, and major trading partner. This central paradox of Canada's existence, the tussle between anti-Americanism and continentalism, has shaped and defined our history. Maintaining our access to the huge market to our south and keeping that access as free and as unfettered as possible is a vital interest for Canada. For that reason, Canada pushed for the Free Trade Agreement of 1989 with the United States and, a few years later, agreed to the inclusion of Mexico in the North American Free Trade Agreement. Canada lives by its trade, and it is clear that no Canadian government can ignore the United States or its rich market. What is also obvious is that deliberately fostering difficulties with Washington, consciously insulting its leaders and attacking its policies, is fundamentally stupid and destructive to the national interest.

At the same time, Canada's ability to influence the United States is largely determined not by our super moralism, as some might believe, but by our readiness to assume a share of responsibility for decisions we will help to make. Political scientist Douglas Ross of Simon Fraser University was blunt: "Largely because of Canada's 15-year-long extraction of a deficit-fighting 'peace dividend' from the Canadian Forces, Ottawa's ability to influence American grand strategy choices is minimal to nil." If you can't play, in other words, no one cares what you might think.

There is one additional point that ties together Canada's vulnerable economy and its defences in the American context. As Colonel Richard Cohen observed in a paper prepared for the Senate's Standing Committee on National Security and Defence, an attack on the United States by terrorists with a Canadian connection would have "a catastrophic effect on our prosperity. Even a relatively minor incident would be enough to severely restrict cross-border trade" for weeks or months. American companies with significant "just in time" delivery facilities in Canada might well close up shop and move back across the border. "A sharp fall in the standard of living of almost every Canadian would certainly follow." It is vital that Canada not allow such an event to occur.

Finally, Canada is not an island, immune from the strife that torments the world. Canadians understand their connectedness, and they realize that their small country must work with like-minded nations to defend freedom and democracy and to advance those great ideals. Canadians went to war in 1914, 1939, 1950, 1991, 1999, and 2002 for democracy and freedom. They cooperate with the United States in defending North America because they are both free and democratic states; and they joined NATO in 1949 because the fate of the European democracies was then, and still is, central to our survival. Our freedoms unite us all. Canada, in other words, cannot be a neutral, and its national interest demands that it work with other states to defend its basic way of life, its place in Western civilization, and, above all, global security.

Those interests are keys to Canadian survival, and we neglect them at our peril. Every prime minister instinctively understands this balancing act, but prime ministers are politicians. They know that if they don't win elections, nothing they say matters. And to win elections, our politicians historically have been prepared to say almost anything, even if their words fly in the face of Canadian national interests.

* * *

My concentration on basic national interests, while it is deliberately meant to raise interests above values, is not meant to downplay the latter. Values matter—for nations every bit as much as for individuals—and just as we all prefer to deal with people who are trustworthy and kind, so nations prefer to deal with other states that ordinarily play by the rules, obey international law, and do not connive and plot against their neighbours.

But how do we project our values onto the world stage? The Chrétien government's 1995 foreign policy White Paper proclaimed that Canada was in a unique position to promote its values of "tolerance, the rule of law and thoughtful compromise" around the world. To implement this policy the following January, Chrétien named Lloyd Axworthy as his Foreign Minister. A doctoral graduate trained in political science at Princeton University, Axworthy was on the nationalist left of the Liberal Party, and he always held strong views on how Canada should deal with and differentiate itself from the United States. It was not so much that this idealist was overtly anti-American but that he pressed values-laden positions that the Americans rejected.

Axworthy believed in "soft power," a phrase coined by Harvard University professor Joseph Nye to describe "co-opting people" but not "coercing" them. The Americans, Axworthy believed, tended to rely on coercion, while Canada, without the military power to coerce nations and peoples, needed to co-opt peoples into doing good. And the good Axworthy hoped to deliver was "human security." This phrase, along with another one, "responsibility to protect," became the hallmarks of Axworthian foreign policy. Human security suggested that the key duty of states was to save peoples and communities rather than concentrating on the defence of borders. The responsibility to protect (R2P) implied that nations could and should come together to impose their will on rogue states and on religious or tribal groups that engaged in genocide or grossly abused their populations.

In an address to the UN Commission on Human Rights in April 1996, Axworthy argued for "a new agenda around the definition of individual security." State borders had become "porous," he said, national defence was of lessening importance, and members of civil society had begun "contacting each other directly and shaping the agenda of their governments" to focus more directly on the prevention and alleviation of human suffering. By "civil society," he meant individuals and non-governmental organizations, for he believed that foreign policy was no longer the preserve of diplomats alone. Vital decisions should not, indeed, could not, be taken without consulting those affected by them. "Let us move the system," Axworthy said, "from one that is based solely around the interests, priorities and responsibilities of states to one that responds to those of the citizenry as well." But who had elected non-governmental organizations to make and deliver foreign policy? That was not a question the Minister wanted to hear or answer. What was certain was that his policy approach placed values high on the agenda and implicitly diminished national interests. Given the primacy of the United States in Canada's interests, this outcome was inevitable. As Allan Gotlieb noted caustically, "never in the history of Canada's foreign relations had differentiation from the United States become a greater imperative than under Axworthy's stewardship."

Axworthy pressed successfully for an anti-personnel land-mine ban and argued, with equal success, for an International Criminal Court that could try genocidal dictators. Who could object to such things? Canadians asked. Unfortunately, the land-mine ban was rejected by all the major powers, notably Russia, China, and the United States,* and no rogue states, failed states, terrorist groups, or guerrilla movements even acknowledged the ban.† Attempts by the Clinton administration to broker a compromise that the United States military and Congress could accept failed. Similarly, the International Criminal Court infuriated many in the United States (and some ninety other nations that refused to accede to it) who feared, correctly, that it might be used for politically motivated proceedings that could single out Americans in many parts of the

*As Paul Chapnick argued in *International Journal* in 2003, Axworthy used an aggressive unilateralist "take it or leave it" bargaining strategy in pushing the land-mines ban, one that created a coalition of the willing because the public wanted results. Very un-Canadian that, especially in the light of the way Canada argued for multilateralism in the 2003 run-up to the Iraq War.

†The Improvised Explosive Devices used to kill Canadians in Kandahar are for all practical purposes anti-personnel mines. To my knowledge, no one has called for the Taliban leadership to be tried by the ICC for employing IEDs.

world.* Moreover, the ICC could launch proceedings against nations and their leaders for actions taken in their national interests. Such an unprecedented attack on state sovereignty could, for example, put the nations that joined in the Kosovo war in 1999, a campaign not sanctioned by the UN Security Council, in the dock. Could that include Lloyd Axworthy, the Canadian Foreign Minister who accepted Canadian participation in the war and who, in his memoirs, conceded that "the actions in Kosovo contravened fundamental articles of national sovereignty without explicit authorization from the UN Security Council"?† Or Paul Heinbecker, the diplomat who had a large hand in crafting Canadian and alliance policy towards the Kosovo conflict? Could it, as Roy Rempel asked in his book *Dream Land*, also lead to an unfriendly nation launching actions against individual Canadian soldiers seconded to the United States or United Kingdom militaries in the similarly unapproved Iraq War after 2003?

The values-based soft-power policies advocated by Axworthy received good reviews almost everywhere except where it mattered most to Canada: in the United States. Was that a net gain for Canada? How did the Minister's activities advance Canadian national interests? To ask such questions does not

*"Should Canada Indict Bush?" the *Toronto Star*'s Tom Walkom asked in November 2004. It could under Canada's "Crimes against Humanity and War Crimes Act," which puts Canadian law in line with the International Criminal Court. Walkom obviously hoped that Bush might be charged in Canada, a reaction as predictable as snow in winter.

†Given that Spain launched proceedings against former Chilean dictator Augusto Pinochet, that is not completely far fetched. Pinochet was a monster with blood on his hands, but it should be up to the Chilean courts to deal with him.

mean that Canada ought not to advance initiatives. It does mean that realism needs to prevail, along with a recognition of what former Liberal Deputy Prime Minister Anne McLellan has called the Americans' "burden of primacy . . . the burden the United States of America carries every day as the world's only superpower and world's leading democracy." If that sole superpower cannot be brought to support a Canadian initiative, our leaders should, at the least, consider closely if they should proceed.

Axworthy's human-security policy agenda was driven by values and morality. It was also—and almost everything Axworthy has said and written since he left the government in 2000 confirms this view—sharply anti-American, and it was assessed as such in Washington by Democratic administrations. Harry Truman's Secretary of State Dean Acheson once wrote of Canada as the "Stern Daughter of the Voice of God." Lloyd Axworthy was the Stern Daughter's moralistic offspring, telling the world what to do and how to do it—at the same time that the governments of which he was a member slashed the Canadian Forces and reduced its capacity to play any major role in cleaning up the world's messes. For too many in Washington, London, and other capitals, Canada talked loudly, carried a very small stick, and always left the hard work to others. Ottawa lost all its credibility with its key allies. Soft power, morality, and an array of values might sound like good policy, but they cannot be all that a nation deploys. Moreover, Canada, a small soft-power nation, cannot change the world by itself or even by cooperating with the Scandinavians and the Dutch. Certainly, Canada's values alone are not enough.

And just what are Canada's key values? To me, they do not include most of those that Minister Graham listed in his consultation paper. Yes, those who make our policy should be sensitive to multiculturalism and be bilingual. The nation's policy-makers should be reflective of the population, and soon, as recent immigrants get Canadian credentials, they will be. But equality, diversity, advocacy of human rights, the rule of law, gender equality, and good governance? Those are all worthy values to which other nations like the Dutch and Scandinavians aspire, as do we (though to judge by our record in some of those areas, our aspirations do not reach very far), but it is patronizing in the extreme to suggest that we will carry those flaming ideals to the unenlightened and downtrodden of the globe. That's a policy for missionaries preaching a twenty-first-century gospel, not a policy for a nation that never even comes close to meeting its foreign-aid targets. And just as I resent missionaries selling the heathen another and better god, so I dislike nations or civilizations pronouncing their values the best and urging others to adopt them. I do think Western values and Western civilization are the most successful, but it is up to others to decide whether they want to adopt them without our preaching at them.

But buried in Bill Graham's list of values are the key ones that do matter to us as we look at the world. Canadian society, he said, is "free, open, prosperous and democratic." I would add to this listing that Canada is a secular and pluralist nation. Those values are critical ones, and they are not merely Canadian but Western. The democratic West has survived and prospered precisely because it is an open society where elections are decided by the enfranchised nation, not just a few. The West is prosperous because its economies are open; it is prosperous because its societies allow talent to rise and do not overly constrain enterprise; and the West is successful because religion, here, does not control the nation-state. The West has freedom of religion, and rightly so, but it also has freedom from religion. Our leaders can pray all they wish, but for a few centuries now they have tended to separate the practices of the state from the tenets of their church. That is not the case in much of the world, particularly the least successful parts of it.

Thus, for Canada, and for every nation, interests are critical, tempered by values. No one would want Canada to decide that its national interest demanded that it seize Greenland because the Inuit there pose a "military" threat or because they are ethnically similar to Canada's Inuit and therefore belong in "Greater Canada." A wholly *realpolitik* view of the world conceivably might suggest such action. That's the point at which values come into play. As a democratic and free society, what justifications could we offer to the world—and, more important, to ourselves—for an invasion? The Canadian media, free and open, would denounce any government that planned such an adventure, and the Opposition in the House of Commons would be in an uproar. Moreover, the record of the last century suggests very strongly that democratic states do not fight wars against other democratic states, and Greenland, harmless as it is, is linked to Denmark, a Canadian ally in NATO for almost six decades. No invasion, thanks. If we ever have serious issues with Greenland, the national interest can and should be pushed aside, and a values-driven agenda should take over. That does not mean that we don't negotiate toughly with Greenland to try to get what we want; it simply means that we do not threaten to bomb the capital city.

But if, say, a newly aggressive Russia decided that the Arctic Islands painted red on our maps really belonged to it, then different issues might come into play. In this scenario, the Russians send in "scientists" accompanied by Spetsnaz special forces armed with powerful weapons. A six-man patrol of Canadian Rangers, the Inuit scouts who constitute much of Canada's presence in the Arctic, go to investigate on their snowmobiles, carrying with them their old unloaded Lee-Enfield .303 rifles, and the Russians kill or capture them. A reconnaissance aircraft has missiles fired at it, and the Russian Embassy in Ottawa begins issuing harsh *démarches* demanding that Canada clear out of the Arctic Archipelago.

If such events were to happen, this would not be the time for a values-driven policy. The nation's key national interests, the security of its territory and its people, would be at stake. The government would ask the United States for assistance, invoking our military alliance of 1940; it would go to NATO in Brussels and call for the collective security provisions of the 1949 treaty to be put in force; it would go to New York and demand that the United Nations Security Council order Moscow out of the Canadian North; and National Defence Headquarters would begin the deployment of Canadian Forces into the Arctic. All Canadians would hope that this dispute could be settled amicably with a Russian withdrawal, apology, and compensation, but if it could not, Canada and its allies might need to fight. Russia is not a free, open, democratic society, and it never has played by the same rules that Canada and similar countries do. Many in Canada almost certainly would call for a compromise—with MPs like Jack Layton, Alexa McDonough, and Ujjal Dosanjh declaring roundly that the

Arctic islands are not worth the bones of a single Canadian grenadier. Let the Russians have half the North, they would say, and let a UN peacekeeping force patrol the rest. But most Canadians would be infuriated by such aggression and would demand action by Ottawa and its allies. Any government that refused to act to protect basic national interests would not survive an election.

Sometimes governments get confused about interests and values. When the Chrétien government was deciding whether to support the United States and Britain in a war against Saddam Hussein in 2003, the Cabinet tried to follow a multilateralist policy, in effect saying that Canada would not support the war unless the United Nations Security Council gave its approval. Canada raised multilateralism to the level of a national interest on this issue by making it clear that the UN Security Council, with France, Russia, and China among its veto-casting members, would determine Canada's position whatever that decision might be. The French and Russians at least shaped their position on Iraq in terms of their national interests, but Canada decided to stand on process in a bogged-down Security Council. Foreign Minister Bill Graham explained: "We would have preferred being able to agree with our close friends and allies . . . However . . . the decision must always be consistent with Canada's long-standing values and principles: in this case . . . that the use of force must always be the last resort of states and our commitment to working through multilateral institutions to resolve questions of peace and security."

That Canada had not always followed this rule was clear, as in the Kosovo war just four years earlier. That it was a pledge to a deeply flawed process in a grossly dysfunctional Security

Council was also clear. And that Canada had previously promised its support—in the eyes of the Bush administration—was swept off the board. For what? For a commitment to multilateralism that, while it had often been a preferred way for Canada to operate, had never been a Canadian national interest, principle, or value. Multilateralism was a tactic, used when it could help constrain great powers and tossed away whenever Canada preferred to paddle its own canoe.

If Canada needed the relationship with the United States to work for both economic and security reasons, this choice on the Iraq War was deeply flawed. No one in Washington expected Ottawa to make anything more than a token commitment to the war, given the state of the Canadian Forces. Thus, for the sake of multilateralism, a tactic raised to the level of a principle or a deeply felt value, Canada risked its national interests. Certainly, national interests must drive some issues, just as values drive others; in this case, the government was simply confused about what mattered most or, more likely, driven by its ministers' anti-Americanism and domestic political considerations.

Ideally, interests and values mesh seamlessly, as our values help to shape the way we pursue our interests. Interests, however, are permanent, etched in stone forever, though the emphasis on one over another may vary over time. Values, in contrast, are substantially more transitory and can also change rapidly. Gender equality may be a present-day value, but it wasn't one believed in by the government or the people in 1920, 1940, or even 1960. Our values of freedom and democracy, however, are integral to Western civilization, and they are both long-lived and vital to us.

In Canada, today, the idea that this country actually has national interests has largely slipped off the government and the public radar. We have touted our values so long and so loudly that the concept of national interests has all but disappeared. One of the tasks of government is to educate the public, and we desperately need a new emphasis on national interests.

Fortunately, there are at last some positive signs. The Canadian Defence and Foreign Affairs Institute paper on national interests found an echo in the Paul Martin administration's International Policy Statement of 2005 and its call for "a clear-eyed understanding of our core national interests." That was a remarkable change from the values-laden policy approach of the Liberal government of Jean Chrétien. Martin is gone now, but the new Harper Conservative government of 2006 has also talked of national interests. On his visit to Afghanistan, his first trip abroad in office, Prime Minister Stephen Harper spoke on March 13 to troops at Kandahar: "You have put yourself on the line to defend our national interests . . . Your work is important because it is in our national interest to see Afghanistan become a free, democratic, and peaceful country." The values Harper spoke about were the important ones of democracy and freedom as touchstones of Canadian policy. That is all to the good, in my view.

I know this interests-based approach will sound harsh, perhaps even too American, to some Canadians. Still, it is true that Canada, like the United States, is both North American and part of the West. Our values are closer together than those of any two powers elsewhere. Our national interests sometimes differ—the United States is Canada's biggest problem, and the reverse is simply not true—but not always. Our security and theirs go together; our economic systems are very similar; and our beliefs in democracy and freedom are the same.

What Canadians need to do is to develop a stronger, clearer focus on what really matters to them. This evaluation is long overdue. Protect our people and our territory. Stand up for our sovereignty, our unity, and our independence. Act in ways that improve Canada's economic viability and the prosperity of its citizens. And cooperate with like-minded nations to advance the progress of freedom and democracy. These goals—and not the constant moralizing about our values and the pretentious rhetoric that we are holier than everyone else—form the recipe for our survival.

Granted, it is sometimes difficult to be clear about national interests in a complex world. Does acting in Afghanistan serve the advance of democracy? Does it help us achieve our objectives with the United States or, as Paul Heinbecker queries, does identifying with American policy endanger Canada? Does the commitment weaken the already-stretched military? It is difficult to decide, no doubt about it. But the simple act of using a national-interest calculus can clear the mind and focus both the government and the public on what matters. Naturally, some will want to act, and some won't. Government must decide, but if our leaders talk national interests to Canadians, they will at the very least provide a sensible rationale for the choices they select. And that can only improve the public's knowledge and the government's decision-making.

We are at war, and we must win it. Ultimately, the war against Islamist terrorism is our war, and the only guide to deciding properly how Canada should play its part is to act to protect and advance the country's national interests.

[4]

Getting on with Washington and the Pentagon

"U.S. Sucks! U.S. Sucks!" That was the chant from the crowd at the World Junior Hockey Championship in Vancouver at the beginning of January 2006. Had it been Canada playing the Americans, such behaviour might have been barely tolerable. But the Canadians weren't on the ice. Instead, it was the United States versus Russia, and the crowd was cheering not *for* the Russians (who won and would next face Canada) but *against* the United States. And, as *Vancouver Sun* reporter Pete McMartin noted on January 5, "the chanters weren't so much interested in a hockey game as scoring points against America the country, not the team." McMartin added that he might have thought he was at an anti–World Trade Organization demonstration. "When the hockey louts start chanting the same slogans as the local Trotskyist cell, you know you have an ugly trend."

Hockey matters to Canadians. In a not-very-nationalistic country, it's one of the few subjects that unites a disparate and regionally—and linguistically—divided nation. Hockey is our game, and no one wants to make too much of a crowd fuelled by beer and a species of patriotism. But Canada is also a country with a professed public devotion to multiculturalism and tolerance, and with stringent laws against hate speech. If the youthful crowd in Vancouver had been chanting "Sri Lanka Sucks!" or "Germany Sucks!" it is possible that the police and the media would have taken a hard line. "U.S. Sucks!" in contrast, drew only one newspaper's notice and hardly merited public attention because the sentiment it expressed is widespread in Canada. The United States is the whipping boy. Opinion polls during recent elections showed Canadian youth to be strongly anti-American; polls of ageing baby boomers demonstrated that they were also more anti-American than they had been in their twenties. So who in Canada is not anti-American? Historians? Governments? Diplomats? We all are, to Canada's detriment.

In my considered opinion, George W. Bush is the worst President of the United States since Warren Harding at the beginning of the 1920s. Ignorant, ill-informed, stubborn, and in hock to the oil industry and big business, his legislative record, his economic and environmental stewardship, and his complete failure in saving lives in hurricane Katrina and in the reconstruction of New Orleans have been disastrous. So, too, most Canadians believe, have been his unilateralist foreign policies, not least the war in Iraq. He sought to make the world safe from terrorism, but instead made the world more unstable, the terrorists more numerous, and, arguably, America weaker. At the same time, his administration's inept actions led to an Iraq that, while free of Saddam Hussein, teeters on the edge of civil war. I am appalled by his administration's use of torture, extraordinary rendition, the abuses at Guantanamo Bay and Abu Ghraib prisons, and a host of violations of the democratic rights and freedoms for which the United States had always stood—until Bush's presidency.

I can make these criticisms, and no one much cares. If I were prime minister of Canada, a Cabinet member, a member of parliament, however, or even press secretary to the prime minister, and I said similar words in the hearing of a journalist, all hell would break loose, and rightly so. Certainly that was the response when Jean Chrétien's press secretary described Bush as a "moron"—and the subsequent reluctant firing of the aide was both deserved and necessary. Leaders of a great neighbouring nation, even brainless leaders, are entitled to receive a degree of public respect from their peers. That is especially so if your country is dependent on the United States for its economic success and ultimate defence. That dependency for Canada is permanent, or at least as permanent as anything can be in a world in flux.

The point is that Bush will be gone in January 2009, to be replaced by another president with (we hope) a different agenda. But Canada's interests, Canada's dependency on the United States, will remain. Presidents come and go, but Canada's national interests remain the same, and Canadians simply must get on with their neighbour, as cordially and constructively as possible. Canadians today have largely forgotten that they were unhappy with President Harry Truman's threats about using nuclear weapons in Korea, President John F. Kennedy's abortive Bay of Pigs invasion of Cuba, President Lyndon Johnson's bombing in Vietnam, and President Richard

Nixon's bombings of Cambodia. They didn't like President Ronald Reagan's invasion of Grenada, and President Bill Clinton's attack on a milk factory in Sudan (because he thought it was being used by al-Qaeda terrorists) upset others.

The public detestation of George W. Bush fits in well with the continuing and widespread anti-Americanism and the habit of disagreeing vehemently with U.S. policy.* Canadians, as historian Frank Underhill said many years ago, are the first anti-Americans, the ideal anti-Americans, the anti-American as he exists in the mind of God. It's true, and it doesn't matter who is president. Nor does it matter, apparently, what Canada's national interests are—and that is the danger.

Now, if you accept that national interests ought to determine Canada's foreign policy—and you should do so because both your job and your nation's security depend on it—then the necessity for getting on with the United States should be clear. For a variety of reasons, historical and contemporary, however, Canadians have trouble dealing with their neighbour.

Why? Because anti-Americanism was the founding myth in Canada, and it remains the state religion—accepted, tolerated, and even encouraged. Multiculturalism may have made racism and xenophobia unwelcome, but anti-Americanism remains intact. Journalist Robert Fulford noted that anti-Americanism gives Canadians "a polite and acceptable form of bigotry. People who would die of shame before tolerating homophobia,

*A poll by the Canada Institute of the Woodrow Wilson International Center in Washington, released in early October 2006, found slowly growing rapport between Canada and the United States. Significantly, however, 63 percent of Americans called Britain America's best friend, while only 17 percent named Canada.

racism or anti-Semitism will cheerfully join in" denouncing the Yanks. Nora Jacobson, an American medical sociologist living in Toronto, wrote angrily in the *Washington Post* in November 2004: "It would be impossible to say things about any other nationality that Canadians routinely say—both publicly and privately—about Americans." She and Fulford are certainly correct. So too is Jacobson's point that, "on a human level, it can be rude and hurtful." Naturally enough, anti-Americanism fluctuates over time and it can be policy specific—the Iraq War, for example, raised the level and amount of abuse substantially. But it is also a constant refrain in the Canadian discourse, a "dissing" of the Yanks individually and collectively that scarcely ever stops.

Canadian nationalism, both historically and to a substantial extent today, is anti-Americanism and anti-imperialism writ large, from Quebec City to Toronto to Vancouver. In the 2005–6 election campaign, Prime Minister Paul Martin seized the occasion of a global conference in Montreal on the Kyoto Treaty to attack the United States for not signing on and for lacking a "global conscience," even though signatory Canada's record of reducing harmful emissions was worse than its neighbour's. "It may be smart election-year politics to thump your chest and constantly criticize your friend and your No. 1 trading partner," rejoined the U.S. Ambassador tactlessly and correctly. "But it is a slippery slope, and all of us should hope that it doesn't have a long-term impact on the relationship."*

*In a submission to the Liberal Party's renewal commission in October 2006, Frank McKenna, who had served as Ambassador in Washington for Prime Minister Martin, said: "Our relationship with the U.S. must be characterized by maturity and confidence. Canadian political leadership must help form Canadian public opinion on the importance of the relationship. Our credibility will be

Martin's remarks were astounding, and although the election campaigning was relatively mild in its expressions of anti-Americanism (compared to, say, 1891, 1911, 1963, or 1988), the *Washington Post*'s Anna Morgan, amazed by the unpleasant tone she discovered on her visit here to cover the campaign, reported that "the United States and all its evils" were a "familiar demon" being employed "to heat Canadian voters to a frenzy."* As Professor David Haglund of Queen's University observed, it didn't take much to turn Paul Martin into Hugo Chavez, and if one of the basic laws of Canadian politics was not to get too close or too far from the Yanks, Martin had badly miscalculated his distance. Robert Fulford noted in the *National Post* that Prime Minister Martin "was sure the Americans wouldn't mind. Most Americans wouldn't notice and those who did wouldn't care. By tradition, the Americans look the other way when Canadian nationalist politicians beat up the U.S. during an election campaign." But when the U.S. Ambassador in Ottawa delivered a speech urging civility, Martin again whacked the Americans—to the glee of French- and English-speaking Canadians and much of the media. The rhetoric didn't win the election for the Liberals—the utter ineptitude of the Prime Minister was such that nothing could—but it likely made the result closer than it otherwise would have been.

greatly enhanced if we save our disagreements for matters of great importance. Picking a fight with our American neighbours for the sake of political expediency undermines our credibility and our influence in important matters."

*It's not just at election time. A Macleans.ca online poll in mid-July 2006 asked readers which country posed the greatest threat to world peace. The respondents voted Iran, 20 percent; North Korea, 23 percent; Russia, 4 percent; and the United States, 51 percent.

Josef Joffe, the editor of the German newspaper *Die Zeit*, has written shrewdly in his book *Überpower* on European anti-Americanism, and his comments ring true in Canada as well. Disagreeing with American policy is one thing, Joffe says, but to denounce the policy simply because it comes from the United States is another. America gets it coming and going—at once puritanical and self-indulgent, philistine and elitist, ultra-religious and excessively materialist. When the United States does not intervene, as in Rwanda, it's wrong; when it does, as in Iraq, it's wrong. Sound familiar?

Anti-Americanism obviously matters in Canada. It is our national *idée fixe.* It always has been and, I suspect, it always will be. In my book *Yankee Go Home? Canadians and Anti-Americanism,* published in 1996, I suggested that "anti-Americanism is weaker in Canada now than ever before . . . the Free Trade election of 1988 . . . [was] the last gasp of a once powerful motivating force." I was wrong.

* * *

Canada's national interests demand that the country protect and enhance its independence. To do so, Canada must strive to resist the pull of the United States, the only nation that threatens our independence—in a benign way, thus far in the twenty-first century*—through the attractiveness of its culture and institutions and the power of its corporations. This resistance

*Some Canadians believe that the United States remains a military threat. In a TV debate with me, Professor Stephen Clarkson said that the United States had already invaded Canada twice and might do so again. Yes, I replied, but that was two hundred years ago (1775 and 1812–14). The time gap didn't appear to matter to Clarkson.

is very hard to accomplish, primarily because the Canadian national interest also demands that we work with the United States to defend North America. The United States protects Canada from external threats and has done so formally since 1940, through the Permanent Joint Board on Defence. Canada accepted reciprocal obligations in this Ogdensburg deal, most notably to ensure that no threat to the United States be mounted from Canadian territory or through Canada because of its weak defences. Some Canadians and many Americans might argue that this obligation has frequently not been met. Certainly, if the Canadian Forces were devoted wholly to neutralist peacekeeping, they could not fulfill these Canadian duties to the United States. The implications of this breakdown—the United States in its own national interests assuming complete responsibility for the defence of all the territories to its north—would be completely destructive of Canadian independence and sovereignty. For Canada, the sole option is to cooperate meaningfully with the United States in defence or to see the Americans assume full responsibility for continental defence—whether we like it or not.

At the same time, Canada must trade with the Americans if it is to remain prosperous. We must balance the need to be independent with the need to be able to live in security and to prosper. Be as independent as possible, of course, but, for Canada, the only choice is to trade with the United States or to see most of our people eating nettles to survive.

This threat from and dependence on the superpower next door inevitably breeds hostility. Anti-Americanism in Canada dates back more than two centuries, and it ebbs and flows with events. It has been very powerful in the years since the end of the Second World War, and many of its most explosive manifestations have come from military questions. Consider the controversy over the stationing of U.S. Air Force technicians on the Distant Early Warning Line in the 1950s, over nuclear weapons in 1962–63, over the Vietnam War in the 1960s and 1970s, over Star Wars during the Reagan years, over the Gulf War, and, most recently, over the war in Iraq. The last, combined with the incredible force of Canadian detestation of President George W. Bush and his administration, has raised anti-Americanism in Canada to perhaps historic peaks. Poll after poll makes clear that Canadians, presumably including Prime Ministers Chrétien and Martin who went out of their way to pander to Canadian anti-Americanism, fear American leadership and policy. The Americans have their own national interests, and today they believe, rightly, that terrorists everywhere are plotting ways to kill Americans. The United States has demonstrated it will do what it deems necessary to protect its interests. Sometimes, the Americans will make terrible mistakes, and Canadians will always line up to let them know that they're wrong.

It is not unusual for a small power living next to a great power to worry about its survival, its culture, its differentness. The Poles perch uneasily between Russia and Germany and have been overrun by one or the other (and sometimes both) repeatedly. The Danes live uneasily next to Germany, and Vietnam is situated on a long border with China, which has used force to achieve its aims. But few nations are so intertwined as Canada and the United States.

The economic links, in particular, are extraordinary. American investment in Canada amounts to $228 billion, two-thirds of all foreign investment, and Canadian investment in the United States is some $165 billion. In 2004, the last year with complete, verifiable data, almost $2 billion a day in Canadian trade went south—some 80 percent of Canada's export trade. The United States provided two-thirds of Canada's imports. The exports amounted to $23,500 for each Canadian, or 52 percent of the nation's gross domestic product, and the Canadian trade surplus with the United States was $94 billion. Incredibly, nine of the ten provinces sell more to the United States than they do to the rest of Canada. As Pamela Wallin, the former Canadian Consul General in New York City, noted, Canada exports more to Home Depot in the United States than it does to France. More than four in ten Canadian jobs depend on this trade, and Canada is incomparably more dependent on its neighbour than the United States is on Canada. Only 5 percent of the United States' gross domestic product comes from trade with us.

We are stuck in an irreversible situation—which is how some Canadians see it, gnashing their teeth. Or we are attached to the engine of global prosperity—which is how others view it. The one key point is that Canada shares a continent with the United States. As such, the links of trade and infrastructure (bank machines, oil pipelines, airlines, computer networks) have been, and are, huge and growing.

There are no prospects for changing this situation, even if Canada should want to do so. Our trade with China, the Communist dictatorship that is frequently touted as Canada's greatest market of the future,* is now just about $36 billion a

*A Strategic Counsel poll in September 2006 found 58 percent of respondents agreeing that, in twenty years, Asian trade will be more important to Canada than U.S. trade.

year—or the equivalent of eighteen days of Canada-U.S. trade. Canada, moreover, has long had a trade deficit with China. India is the other nation usually projected to be an economic giant. Canadian exports to the Indian subcontinent are, regrettably, almost negligible, amounting in 2005 to $3 billion, or 0.6 percent of Canadian trade. Canadian trade with the world's second most populous state amounts to one-and-a-half day's trade between Canada and the United States. The total Asian trade makes up only 12 percent of our exports.

Naturally, Canadians want to increase their trade with Asia, with Latin and South America, with Europe—indeed, with everyone. But a dash of realism is needed. There is simply no realistic possibility in the next half-century of increasing the China or the India markets sufficiently to replace trade with the United States. Most Canadians have forgotten that in the 1970s, Ottawa struck deals with the European Community and Japan in an effort to reduce Canada's dependence on the American market. The effort failed miserably, not least because Canadian manufacturers and exporters found it difficult to break into new markets speaking different languages and with different standards. They preferred the familiar, reliable, rich, English-speaking United States. In fact, why would the government even want to try to diversify?* How is it that so many Canadians believe that the huge advantage provided by their proximity to the United States' market is a national liability?

* * *

*That is the conclusion of one of the papers in *NAFTA@10*, published in 2006 by the Department of Foreign Affairs and International Trade.

Given Canada's economic dependency, it's curious how Canadians still believe that their expression of detestation for their neighbour will not matter. Issues such as softwood lumber, which might have been resolved in the past by intervention in Congress or in the departments by the president and the Executive Branch, seemed to drag on forever, yet the public never seemed to connect them to popular or Canadian government expressions of disdain for the United States. Pamela Wallin, watching from New York City, thought not only that Canadian politicians had made mistakes but that there were additional effects as well. There were "economic consequences," she said, "not the shut-down of a plant but investment decisions favouring Canada were not made. This is only logical. If you are at war or under siege and you have to choose between a plant in Canada and one in Tennessee, you're going to favour the home team." David Jones, a former senior American diplomat who served in Ottawa and who speaks out with increasing bluntness, similarly warned of what he called the "residual resentment" in the United States at the "shiftless brother-in-law, when you know he will never pull his weight . . . Canadians," he went on, "continue to assume that the U.S. will remain benign, and the essential elements of their sovereignty will remain intact." But, Jones said, it might no longer be so.

On one level, a modicum of anti-Americanism is necessary for Canadian survival. Canada is the North American "other," a nation that was founded on being different and still strives to be so. Canadian social policies, for example, are different from those of the United States, and so are our institutions and forms of government. Some values appear to be different, perhaps increasingly so, and those who hold them want to keep them. These distinctions, this sense that there is a different way of doing things in Canada, form the legitimate side of Canadian anti-Americanism, or what we might call Canadian-not-being-Americanness.

Nonetheless, over time, many and perhaps most of the differences between the two North American democracies have disappeared, except for the shouting and posturing against the American political, cultural, and economic imperialists that is so demeaning to those who practise it. Even worse, insulting the nation that guarantees Canadian prosperity and Canadian defence is extremely detrimental to the national interest. Cheap anti-Americanism serves no Canadians' purposes. Chanting "U.S. sucks," calling Bush a "moron," and deliberately kicking a superpower in the shins on issues of vital concern to its leaders and people do nothing to achieve a resolution of Canadian concerns in Washington. Nor do they help make meetings between prime ministers and presidents more harmonious. National interests are critical, but personal relationships can still smooth over tough issues. It is almost certainly fair to say that Chrétien and Martin did not have a warm feeling for President Bush. Did that serve the achievement of Canadian aims and protect the country's national interests? Does Dubya look like a man who forgets who slags him and who doesn't?

Canadians need to realize that the United States is not going to disappear and that Canada is not an island. Geography has made us neighbours, and that is Canada's ace in the hole. Most Canadians don't want to be Americans, but they all need a strong and prosperous United States if their own country is to survive and prosper. Anyone with eyes to see should understand this equation. Canadians also need an engaged United

States dealing with global problems. That too serves our interests—almost all the time.

It may be that the Conservative government in Ottawa will be able to deal sensibly with its superpower neighbour and simultaneously make the achievement of Canada's national interests a more important priority than preaching its allegedly superior values. Maybe. But the powerful strain of anti-Americanism in Canadian life is not going to disappear, and any government that forgets that—and forgets how powerful anti-Americanism can be—does so at risk of its survival.

* * *

During the run-up to the Iraq War in 2003, I made a book tour and appeared on phone-in shows or gave talks in most of Canada's big cities. With the exception of Halifax, still a good navy town, the anti-American bile that spewed out at me was distressing. Part of it was spurred by the widespread sense that President Bush was in thrall to the oil industry and the captive of his Vice-President and Secretary of Defense. Part of it was a sincere belief in the United Nations, multilateralism, and opposition to American unilateralism, though how anyone can pretend that the UN is an effective agency for peace is baffling in the extreme. And part of it completely contradicted the strong Canadian government and public support for R2P, the responsibility to protect peoples from their despotic governments. Freeing Iraq's people from Saddam Hussein did not appear to count as a worthy goal—because the United States was doing the work.

Most of the anti-Americanism I heard was motivated by envy, by hatred and fear, by the sense that Canada somehow was next on the Bush administration's agenda, that Canadian sovereignty was threatened. They want our water and oil, a few said (and they may well be right). They're rich capitalists, pressing globalization, pushing free trade that benefits the United States and hurts everyone else, and they're too damn full of themselves, some argued. The United States armed forces' new Northern Command was a device to take us over militarily, others feared. And, as one student in Montreal commented, it would be better if Canada had no army at all than that the Americans should use Canadian troops in their wars.

Canadians believe they know their neighbours, and not a few will still say that some of their best friends are Americans—and they don't even mind if their daughter marries one. But most Canadians clearly have missed the full extent of the shock caused to the American body politic by September 11. The historic sense of American invulnerability that had grown since the attack on Pearl Harbor on December 7, 1941, was destroyed that day in September 2001 and replaced by fear. If Canadians understood this reaction, they might be more understanding.

Sadly, predictably, Americans have noticed that their neighbour is no longer friendly and always supportive. The conservative Fox News, widely available and hugely influential on cable TV, is now the first ever anti-Canadian TV network, with popular and vicious commentators Bill O'Reilly, Neil Cavuto, and John Gibson leading the way in blasting our "liberal excesses," anti-Americanism, and unreliability as an ally. Cavuto's book, *Hating America*, portrays Canada as "America's France Next Door." "The Canadians can't help themselves," he wrote. "They know the U.S. isn't going to invade them so they feel empowered—if not entitled—to act as self-consciously superior as possible." This malevolent attitude matters, given the way O'Reilly, Cavuto, and Gibson increasingly dominate cable news in the United States, and now in Canada and around the globe as well. It matters because Congress frequently dances to Fox's tune, something the Canadian Embassy in Washington discovered when, as one senior official observed to me, he found Fox News playing in every Congressman's office he entered. The Embassy is now trying to counter this influence by getting the ambassador on-air as quickly as possible to counter Fox's misrepresentations.

Well, so what? Canada is an independent state, and if we choose to differ from the United States on a major issue of war and peace, that's our business. If we choose to run down our military, that's up to us. Besides, the U.S. was wrong in Iraq and we were right, weren't we?

Well, no. I believed that Canada—in its own national interests—should have lent political support to the war against Saddam. (We had very few military assets to commit, but the Americans would have been pleased merely to have a Canadian flag on the coalition's letterhead.) The Iraqi dictator was a monster who had brutalized his people for years, and I thought it was credible that he had weapons of mass destruction. He had, after all, used them against his own Kurdish citizens fifteen years before. As I sometimes tell my granddaughter, the fact that there is no monster under her bed is no guarantee that there aren't monsters out there. There are—and Saddam was one—and the world, including the Iraqi people, is better off without him.

The victory over Saddam's armed forces in the spring of

2003 was quick enough that, for a time, I believed I was right in my analysis, but the subsequent chaos certainly suggests otherwise. I had been wrong to assume that the United States had planned for the post-victory period, wrong to assume that Defense Secretary Donald Rumsfeld had thought to have sufficient troops available to protect museums and government offices and to secure oilfields, arms caches, and strategic points. Incredibly, the United States appeared to believe that no planning was needed, that military victory was sufficient, and that a new Iraqi democracy would automatically spring into being to cheers from Shia, Sunnis, and Kurds. The wanton looting of great museums was the first indicator of the coming chaos. Without doubt, the insurgency that arose might have been prevented or at least curtailed if rational post-battle plans had been in place. The Bush-Cheney-Rumsfeld administration deserves all the opprobrium it has received for the mess it created, and the Republicans fully earned the major defeat they suffered in the 2006 elections.

Still, no one ought to suggest that Jean Chrétien's Ottawa understood what was going to occur in Iraq. The decision to stay out of the war was, in my view, made not because the United Nations Security Council didn't agree to authorize the war and not because the Department of Foreign Affairs had assessed matters correctly. The decision to commit troops to Afghanistan in February 2003* and to stay out of the war in Iraq

*The commitment to Afghanistan in early 2003 was explicitly understood to make it impossible for Canada to fight in Iraq. As Defence Minister John McCallum explained: "The Afghanistan mission is it for Canada. Defence Secretary Donald Rumsfeld welcomed the initiative. Mr. Rumsfeld, I might add, is fully cognizant of the fact that this mission limits the deployment of

came about because of the coincidence of the Quebec provincial election and the fear in Ottawa that a victory by Jean Charest's Liberals might be put in doubt by a decision to support the Americans in Iraq. Getting the Parti Québécois out of power, in other words, was worth upsetting the United States. Perhaps that was true; if it was, Ottawa might have brought the country in on the decision and made Canadians aware that there might be consequences in our dealings with the United States.

What Canadians need now is a stiff dose of *realpolitik*. We can, of course, disagree with George W. Bush's Washington, and we should on occasion, but we must pick our spots carefully. If our direct national interests are involved, we must push as hard as we can and muster allies in Congress and in American statehouses behind us. On non-security issues involving both countries, Canada can be as vocal and as critical as it chooses. Americans argue among themselves too, and they won't be offended. On the softwood lumber dispute, for example, Canada had a major lobbying and legal effort in operation and actively sought allies among home contractors who needed cheap lumber. But when

Canadian land forces to other parts of the world for well over a year." The decision, Lieutenant-General Mike Jeffrey, the Chief of Land Staff at the time, told CBC News in October 2006, was made against his advice and, he added, the government announcement in Parliament on February 12, 2003, took him by surprise: "I did not know . . . that the decision had been made to go." The decision, in other words, was wholly political. Curiously, Eddie Goldenberg's *The Way it Works* (2006), which discusses the Iraq decision at length, makes no mention of the preceding Afghan deployment. The decision to accept the Kandahar deployment in 2005 similarly took place to appease the United States. The Canadian Ambassador to Washington, Michael Kergin, later put it this way: "There was this sense that we had let the side down [in Iraq] . . . and then there was the sense that we could be more helpful, militarily, by taking on a role in Afghanistan."

American administrations believe that their national security is threatened, as they have since September 11, 2001, Canadians should have sense enough to recognize that Washington is a superpower with global concerns that are different from those of our small, weak nation. Canada likes to think itself motivated by higher things than the crass, materialistic, imperialistic United States, but that is fantasy. The Americans, when they think of us at all, see us as an unreliable ally, a nation of carping complainers that regularly fails to carry its weight in the world. Why feed this perception?

Thus, when the United States feels its security is in jeopardy and we disagree, our leaders' dissent should be expressed quietly through diplomatic channels. Anything else, any harsh disagreement or outright wobbling, hurts us immeasurably with Congress, the administration, and the American media. The Chrétien government's "yes I will—no I won't" policy on the Iraqi question and the Martin government's on-off position on Ballistic Missile Defence were perfect examples of pandering to the home folks and squandering political assets south of the border. It wasn't that we said no, Pamela Wallin noted as she left her post in New York, "but how we said no and the name-calling." *Realpolitik*—picking one's spots carefully, saying as little as possible, and doing what one must—is the only way to deal with the giant to our south. We may not be a moral superpower if we practise such a policy, but we will continue to eat and work and prosper.

* * *

There is one legitimate reason for Canadians to worry about the United States: defence. As a superpower, the United States has a huge military, with extraordinary budgets and vast capabilities. The American armed forces can deploy thousands of troops almost anywhere on earth faster than the Canadian Forces can move one of our understrength battalions from Camp Petawawa to Ottawa. (I exaggerate only slightly.) The technological and qualitative gap between American forces and any possible challengers is huge and growing daily.

So why are the Americans so worried? Because "rogue" states such as North Korea or Iran are developing nuclear weapons, long-range missiles, and weapons of mass destruction of a biological or chemical kind. All these materials can threaten the United States and other nations, including Canada. Moreover, despite the unchallenged military power the United States commands, asymmetric warfare allows guerrillas, terrorists, and suicide bombers to strike at the U.S. homeland and its territories, its troops, or its assets at home and abroad. The attacks of September 11 were a perfect example; so too is the Sunni guerrilla resistance in Iraq and the Taliban insurgency in Afghanistan. Security has therefore become the major priority of the Bush administration—and it will also be the top priority for the administration, Republican or Democratic, that succeeds it in January 2009. As political scientist Joel Sokolsky wrote, "this is the hard geopolitical reality that will define bilateral security relations at home and away for years to come."

The implications should be obvious to Canada. Canadians are unhappy about American efforts to erect watchtowers along the border, to tighten border controls, or to require passports or equivalent documents for visitors or citizens returning overland by June 2009. The impact of such regulations on the already slowing Canadian economy and tourist industry is potentially horrendous, as Ottawa, provincial premiers, and border state governors have shouted repeatedly. American businesses will get hurt as well, but U.S. calculations show that most of the pain will occur north of the border. The administration and the Congress in Washington care about the hurt, but not too much. Security is the top priority in an age in which Islamist terrorism is on the rise.* The hoary cliché of "the undefended border" is about to disappear.

Americans also worry about Canada's "soft" policies on immigration and refugees. They are concerned that the large Muslim concentrations in our cities could make them a launching pad for attacks on the United States. Although none of the September 11 terrorists entered the United States from Canada, many Americans continue to believe that they did.† The "Millennium bomber," Ahmad Ressam, did, after all, get into the United States from Canada en route to his attempt to bomb Los Angeles airport. Ressam, an Algerian refugee claimant who lived in Montreal, was, fortuitously, apprehended on December 14, 1999, by a U.S. Customs agent in Washington

*In September 2006 Georgia Congressman Charlie Norwood released a private task-force report that claimed "tens of thousands of illegal immigrants a year" from the Middle East, China, Pakistan, and Thailand came into the United States from Canada. His solution: more than 8,000 troops, Coast Guard, and air patrols, as well as 1,000 more border agents.

†The *Washington Times*, December 21, 1999, had this reaction to the Ressam incident: "U.S. Justice Department officials yesterday said Canada's soft laws on political asylum opened a back door through which suspected terrorist Ahmed Ressam was able to enter the United States last week with bomb-making materials. 'We are concerned by the fact that Canada's laws do facilitate the entry into the United States of individuals who may pose a terrorist threat—even the Canadians recognize that,' said a Justice Department official. 'This relates most directly to their refugee and asylum policies and their general policy of not detaining people.'"

State, his car loaded with explosives and bomb-making equipment. Ressam had links to al-Qaeda, and U.S. anti-terrorism officials were furious that Canadian security agencies had missed him. His capture led to major reviews of U.S. security (though not thorough enough to prevent the September 11 attacks), but, wrote Wesley Wark, Canada's leading intelligence scholar, "no similar effort was made in Canada, despite the centrality of Ressam and the lucky near-miss his case represented."

Attitudes shaped by the Ressam episode and the persistent myth that the September 11 plotters entered the United States over its northern border almost certainly contributed to the attack by New York Senator Hillary Clinton on lax Canadian border security when five men of Middle Eastern appearance turned up on an FBI watch list; they had allegedly entered the United States from Canada. The whole affair proved to be nonsensical, except that Clinton, a likely 2008 Democratic presidential candidate, believed that the Canadian border was a persistent cause of insecurity for Americans. Perhaps as damaging, an episode of *The West Wing* featured President Josiah Bartlett's White House locked down because of a dangerous terrorist who had entered the United States across the "Ontario-Vermont border." As Victoria political scientist Reg Whitaker observed, the writers "assumed that the natural place for a terrorist to enter the U.S. was from Canada." That there is no Ontario-Vermont border didn't seem to matter.* More seriously,

*In mid-2006 the United States had 950 border patrol agents along the Canadian border, compared to 10,200 patrolling the half-as-long Mexican border. To the end of May, 830,000 illegals had been apprehended at the Mexican border, compared to 4,066 at the Canadian. If Senator Clinton believes there are problems, it is in her power to press for an increase in America's northern border protection.

one of the September 11 Commission members and a former congressman, Lee Hamilton, told the Canadian Embassy that "the FBI is more worried about the northern than the southern border," largely because of Muslims from Europe coming to Canada, with most going to Quebec.

Such fears, such events, real and fictional, continue to resonate. One Department of Homeland Security official told a Congressional committee on July 17, 2006, that "terrorists repeatedly try to enter the United States from Canada." In fact, the bureaucrat said, "there are five times the number of terrorist watch list matches on the northern border than there are on the southern border." There are reasons for this discrepancy—tens of thousands of illegals slip across the U.S. border with Mexico each year without screening of any kind—but it is the perception that matters, and the effects this perception has on a wide range of Canadian-American issues. The real threat of terrorism in Canada, of course, is that the United States might begin to believe that it must defend its northern border in a serious way. First, a driver's licence was enough to get a Canadian into the United States; in 2009, it will be a passport; and the year after, who knows? What is beyond doubt is that, if a major terrorist assault on the United States is launched from Canada, the effects will be catastrophic for Canada's relations and trade with its neighbour.

Then there is straight military security. American ambassadors since the 1950s have demanded that Canada do more to protect North America. The level of complaint rose sharply in the 1980s and crested again after the attacks on the World Trade Center and the Pentagon in 2001. In American eyes, Canada is a vast undefended space to their north, a blank area in which there are few military assets beyond some obsolescent

CF-18 jets working with the North American Aerospace Defence Command, a handful of ships on each coast, and small numbers of soldiers. Ever since 1940, the two North American nations have cooperated closely on military questions, but most of the defence has been provided by the United States.

For Canada, the object has always been to provide just enough military capacity to be able to tell Washington that it need have no fear about its northern border and to oblige the United States to plan the defence of the continent in concert with Ottawa. In effect, our policy has been to provide enough defence to keep the Americans out of Canada and to defend us against their help. "We have your back," Ottawa has said, "and no threats to the United States will be permitted to materialize from Canada's air, land, and sea space. So don't worry, and please stay south of the border." Most times, this claim was not wholly accurate, but Canada provided sufficient military resources and cooperated closely enough with the Pentagon that the U.S. military felt more or less reassured. This level of comfort prevailed after the end of the Cold War, when both countries reduced their military forces. But Canada cut budgets and personnel deeper and faster than the Americans did. The budget cuts under the Chrétien government amounted to one-third of defence spending, and the Canadian Forces' strength, equipment, and capabilities collapsed.

The Americans noticed, especially after September 11. They noticed once the Chrétien government decided not to participate militarily in Iraq and declined even to support the United States politically. Why, in the face of this inactivity, should the United States discuss major security questions with Canada? The Americans are indifferent to Canada—unless what we do and don't do threatens them. They watched as Paul Martin's government first sounded as if it would join in Ballistic Missile Defence and then, without even the courtesy of informing Washington directly, decided to opt out for the most crass of domestic political reasons. Those slights—and they were seen as such in the United States—fed into Washington's growing concerns that Canada's defence weaknesses threatened their own continental security.

There are two factors that are contributing to this concern in the United States. The first comes from the U.S. armed forces' view that the capabilities and equipment of the Canadian Forces have atrophied so much that they are no longer interoperable with U.S. forces. Given that, why should the United States share command with Canada in NORAD? As Bernard Stancati wrote in *Parameters*, the journal of the U.S. Army War College: "The reality of the situation, then, is this: if Canada permits doubt to continually creep into the Canada-US defense and security partnership in the post-9/11 environment, it may find itself being slowly ushered out."

The second American concern hinges on the Canadian political will to act. Dr. Stancati noted bluntly that U.S. doubts about Canada could drive the United States to question seriously "whether its northern partner has the political will to pull its share and to do its part to secure the continent from attack. Historical and recent events demonstrate a willingness on the part of the United States to take unilateral action on the continent if it believes such is necessary to protect its own interests. In terms of either a ballistic missile or maritime attack, the possibility exists that the United States would consider defecting from the partnership if Canadian policymaking causes the United States to lose confidence in its partner's willingness, resolve, or ability to take action."

It is not in the Canadian national interest to have the neighbouring superpower harbour such doubts. Nor is it in the national interest to lose the cooperative relationship in defence, because that means one of two things: either Canada pays the full cost of providing defence to a standard that does not cause legitimate concern in the United States or Canada cedes its defence to the United States. The first course is ruinously expensive in cost. The second will be completely destructive to Canadian sovereignty and nationhood.

Canadians have always assumed that the United States would protect them *in extremis*, and that is surely true. America's national interests can never accept that any hostile power entrench itself on Canadian territory. That stance is legitimate and reasonable, not aggressive and overbearing, and Canadians should thank their good fortune that they live next door to the United States, not Germany or Russia. We might have been the Poland of North America, subject to the ruthless demands of aggressive neighbours.*

But what if, as Stancati implies, American national interests some day require the United States to assume full responsibility for the defence of Canadian territory—with or without Ottawa's consent? If Canadian military incapacity is such that the existence of a vacuum to the north of the 49th parallel poses a threat to American national interests, the United States might be forced to act, no matter what Ottawa said or the violation

*In fact, when Britain was a world power with effective forces in or off Canada in the nineteenth century, we were a Poland, subject to threats from the south whenever Washington and London disagreed on serious matters.

of Canadian sovereignty. I doubt that the United States would follow such a course lightly, and, obviously, it would always prefer to have Canadian concurrence in any actions it might take on or over Canadian territory. But necessity knows no law, and it is entirely possible that, under threat, the United States might believe itself forced to act. Indeed, it is almost inevitable. If the United States has to defend us, our independence will be a sham and our sovereignty will have ended. We truly will be a vassal state.

How can such an eventuality be prevented? There is only one way: Canada must genuinely have the military capacity to be able to tell Washington truthfully that the Canadian Forces can stop any threats from reaching the United States from Canadian territory. Our military must be of sufficient size and have the right equipment to be able to counter any possible incursion or to deal with any terrorist threats from the sea, by air, or over land. Obviously, such capacity will protect Canada's population and territory at the same time as it meets the concerns of the United States. The protection of its people is the first priority of every government, and it is one that Ottawa historically has shrugged off. This irresponsibility was never desirable or acceptable, but now, in the age of terrorism, it is no longer possible. Being a sovereign state has certain obligations, and being capable of mounting your own defence is a basic requirement.

Being sovereign, however, does not mean that a nation such as Canada can stand by itself. Too many Canadians, their judgment warped by anti-Americanism, think that the United States is the enemy. It's not. Canada needs the United States to be the effective manager of global security. We must also cooperate closely with Washington in the defence of North America and the approaches to it, and we should, if Dr. Stancati is to be believed, earn recognition once more of our willingness and ability to do so. We will need American help if terrorists blow up downtown Montreal or if there is an earthquake off Vancouver. The Americans will need our assistance if Vermont is hit by an ice storm or if Seattle is devastated by a pandemic. Good neighbours cooperate when their interests mesh. Most of the time, the interests of Canada and the United States are similar.

But there are other, even more frightening possibilities in the twenty-first century. Canada needs to be involved, for example, in Ballistic Missile Defence and whatever other measures the two nations decide are necessary for the defence of the continent. If North Korea, the mad hermit kingdom, ever decides to launch a nuclear missile at North America—and it will soon have the capacity to do so—Vancouver is as much at risk as Seattle, unless Pyongyang has better missile guidance systems than anyone suspects. If the United States fell into a war with China or a newly malevolent Russia, to cite two terrifying possibilities, then Ballistic Missile Defence would be critical to continental defence, both possible opponents being armed with nuclear-tipped intercontinental missiles. We are involved whether we like it or not in such eventualities, and it seems absolutely clear to me that we will have zero influence on continental defence if the Canadian government continues Prime Minister Martin's policy of staying out of this defence.*

*Writing in the *Canadian Military Journal* in 2006, Andrew Richter argued that the Martin decision "stood conventional wisdom on its head." For zero investment, Canada would have received "a seat at the table." "Canada's irrelevance in security matters," he said, "had never been more apparent than

I am a realist on defence and foreign policy questions, and I recognize that the superpower paying the bills and deploying the weaponry will always have the major share of responsibility and decision-making. Any voice at the table, however, is obviously better than none. What sovereignty do we have left if we aren't at the table and the decision to act is made without our voice being heard? What value is our independent right to decide if we don't share in the key decisions that will affect our survival? Hasn't it always been a basic premise since 1940 that, in our own interest, Canada would be a staunch ally of the United States in defence of our common homeland? How was it that this fundamental principle of Canadian foreign policy in the modern era disappeared during the Chrétien-Martin era?

When President Bush and Prime Minister Martin met in January 2005 to discuss Ballistic Missile Defence, among other subjects, the President was genuinely surprised at the Canadian's lack of interest in defence. A Canadian official at the meeting said that Bush commented: "I'm not taking this position, but some future president is going to say, 'Why are we paying to defend Canada?'" The Canadians tried to explain the difficult domestic politics involved, but Bush, not quite

it was at that moment." There was "a disconnect between *declaratory* policies and *actual* policy." Extraordinarily, Martin's government appeared to understand that its BMD decision made no sense: its *International Policy Statement* of 2005 observed that "it is in Canada's national interest to continue to engage cooperatively with the US on measures that directly affect Canadian territory and citizens, and to maintain our ability to influence how the North American continent is defended." Not surprisingly, the Liberal-controlled Standing Senate Committee on National Security and Defence, which has been hawkish on defence for years, in October 2006 called for Canada to join in Ballistic Missile Defence.

as stupid as most Canadians believe he is, waved them off: "I don't understand this. Are you saying that if you got up and said this is necessary for the defense of Canada, it wouldn't be accepted?" There was no answer, but it is no wonder that some in the United States see Canadians as freeloaders on defence for forty years and more, failing to pay their share to defend their North American homeland. Others are simply puzzled that Canada seems determined to turn over responsibility for continental defence to the Americans. Why would they do it? they ask.

Many Canadians will be certain to object that, by doing such things as cooperating in Ballistic Missile Defence, Canada is tying itself to the United States' chariot wheels ever more tightly. Jack Layton will speak sternly about surrendering to the Pentagon's wrong-headed policies and cooperating in a system that does not and cannot ever work, and the Liberal leader will warn that Canada is trampling on the sacred policies enunciated by Mackenzie King, Lester Pearson, Pierre Trudeau, and Jean Chrétien. But such concerns will miss the point entirely. The United States *will* act to protect itself—its national interests demand that it do so—and the only question for Canadians is how best to protect our own interests. Does dismissing American concerns do it? Or does cooperating with the neighbour on whom we depend?

There really should be no debate at all here. Lloyd Axworthy, referring to Ballistic Missile Defence, argued in his memoirs that "further military integration would result in the disappearance of a distinctive Canadian voice in the disarmament debate. We would lose our ability to offer good advice," he went on, "and help influence American thinking. Being an appendage just doesn't carry much weight with Washington." I don't want to make Axworthy a foil in this book, but his utter misunderstanding of reality,* so dangerous because it is pervasive in the Department of Foreign Affairs, the Opposition in the House of Commons, and the media, makes it difficult to neglect him. Disarmament matters, but in the age of terrorists and rogue states that cannot be reined in by anything but force (or so it seems), it is not the most pressing priority for either Washington or Ottawa.

More than specific issues, however, what truly matters is how we approach the United States. Differ loudly from Washington and shun integration and cooperation, as Axworthy prefers? Or cooperate where we can, working together in the areas we must? Turning our back on the United States leaves Washington alone to interpret the requirements of continental defence, and this approach, as I suggested above, means the inevitable diminution of Canadian sovereignty and independence. Lloyd Axworthy hated to see one penny spent on defence, and he detested the idea of working with the United States. Why he could not see that this attitude threw away advantages for our diplomacy and jeopardized our sovereignty is beyond me—

*Mark Proudman, reviewing Axworthy's memoir, observed that the former minister "is a Canadian nationalist, and Canadian nationalists, like the nationalists of many other second-class Western powers, construct their ideology against the putatively bellicose, intellectually simplistic, and morally tainted Americans . . . The nationalists of second-class powers get to have their cake and eat it too: they imagine themselves cosmopolitan internationalists while retaining all the emotional gratifications of national prejudice." Moreover, with North Korea now having nuclear capability, with Iran on the verge of acquiring it, one wonders what is left to debate about disarmament. The Axworthian "distinctive Canadian approach" has been a complete failure.

ideological blinkers, I suppose, do precisely that to America-haters. Cooperation is the only possible course for us to follow. Such a policy is very much in the Canadian national interest because it protects Canadian sovereignty, enhances Canada's independence, and ensures—as much as such assurances can be given—continued access to the markets we depend on.

It is also true, as Rob McRae, one of the draftsmen of the Martin government's *International Policy Statement* of 2005, wrote in an academic article, that "Canada-US relations not only intersect with most domestic issues . . . [but] are an integral consideration to almost every international issue that concerns Canada." The United States matters greatly to us at home and abroad: it is where some of Canada's most critical national interests will be determined, and it should be a basic fact of Canadian governance that prime ministers need to examine issues through an American lens before voicing their opinion or jeopardizing their country's best interests. We simply must get the relationship right, and recent governments have not been very effective here.

This goal does not mean that Canada must always agree with the United States. Our national interests are similar to those of the United States, but they are not identical. We are free to interpret our interests as we wish, and we are not obliged to join in the coming war with Iran, for example. The Americans understand that different countries have different interests and capabilities and, while they might shout at us, they won't bomb Ottawa. But Canadian governments must look at the national interest in making a decision on such a war: What best serves our military and economic security? What helps the advance of democracy most? Participation or abstention? We will always retain the ability to decide what we choose to do and how we decide to do it, but Ottawa has the necessity and the responsibility to weigh the benefits and costs of each decision.

Let me be completely clear on one absolutely critical point: where Canada lacks the freedom to decide is on continental defence. The Americans will defend their territory and interests with every weapon at their disposal. If Canadian governments make mistakes in assessing this nation's interests in this area, then Canadian sovereignty and independence are in serious jeopardy.

* * *

Douglas Fisher, the former New Democratic Party Member of Parliament who turned himself into a fine political columnist, closed out his long writing career on July 30, 2006. In his farewell column, Fisher tried to suggest the major problems Canada faced. Quebec would not separate, he said, and he worried that Canadians bragged too much about "our vast land and our superior ways in health care and peacekeeping"—something that upset him, he said, "because bragging is so un-Canadian." He went on to argue that the "great and immediate question" for the coming decade is "How do we come to sensible, workable terms with the most basic animus now affecting our polity, i.e., our rampant anti-Americanism?" To Fisher, if Canada cannot control this anti-Americanism "and divert its force into a national determination to know our neighbours better and make them understand our grievances better, we could face organized hostility and major troubles from the U.S."

He's right, as right as Fisher almost always was. If it comes to trouble with the United States, Canada cannot win any political war. It might win occasional battles, but the big battalions, as Napoleon knew, invariably had God on their side. It is in Canada's national interest to get on with the United States, and our political leaders must take the lead here and work to diminish the poisonous force of Canadian anti-Americanism. It is no less strong than it has been in the past, and it remains powerful enough, as Fisher forecast, to lead to "organized hostility" south of the border. That hostility, now becoming evident among politicians and in the U.S. media, can only be a disaster for Canada and Canadians. In the war for economic prosperity and national survival, in the war against terror, Canada simply cannot afford to alienate its largest customer, best friend, and ultimate defender.

[5]

True North: Strong, Free, Ours?

Sovereignty is a word Canadians use frequently and, typically, it has different meanings to different Canadians. In French Canada, sovereignty means independence, the shaking off of the oppressive Anglo yoke. English Canadians generally think of sovereignty as a term to describe the state of relations with the United States (as I used it in the previous chapter). In this meaning, we are more or less sovereign depending on the degree of integration we have with the Americans. That, of course, is a dangerous definition because there is little sovereign independence if we are unemployed and starving—and total sovereignty for us means just that.

There is another peculiarly Canadian definition of sovereignty which pertains to the Arctic. There, sovereignty means that the Great White North belongs to us, that it is ours. ("Take off to the great white north," the quintessentially Canadian hosers, Bob and Doug McKenzie, said, "it's a beauty way to go!") Sovereignty, in other words, is ownership of the

Arctic or, as a minimum, the Canadian ability to exercise control over who does what there. In essence, sovereignty means that Canadian laws have jurisdiction.

Most Canadians simply assume that all the Arctic is Canadian. There is even growing support for the idea of changing Canada's motto ("A Mari usque ad Mare") to read "From sea to sea to sea," adding the Arctic Ocean to the existing recognition of the nation's Atlantic and Pacific coasts. But Canadians fail to realize that our claims in the Far North are not universally accepted; that our occupancy of much of the Arctic is non-existent; that Canada has almost no military force or surveillance capabilities in the area; and that the Northwest Passage, which we think of as Canadian (ice) waters, is seen by most powers, including the United States, the European Union, and Japan, as an international strait—exactly as Cape Horn or the Singapore Strait are viewed. Moreover, international law might not be on our side. "Canada's claim to the Arctic Archipelago," said the Canadian Institute of Strategic Studies in 2005, "is tenuous at best."

While almost all the land in the archipelago seems indisputably Canadian, the one place where Canadian sovereignty is actively under attack is Hans Island, a tiny rock of about 1 square kilometre located between Ellesmere Island (Canadian) and Greenland (autonomous but Danish-controlled). In 2003 Denmark indicated that it claimed the island as its own, a position it backed up by sending an ice-capable frigate to land troops for a brief stay on the island. The Danish claim was challenged by Ottawa, which quickly sent its own ships, much less capable of operating in ice than the Danes' vessels, and eventually a helicopter carrying Liberal Defence Minister Bill

Graham to the tiny island to plant the flag. How the dispute will be resolved remains uncertain. Some experts urge that Canada should not seek a resolution, arguing that Ottawa should simply wait out the Danes. This may not be a good idea—Copenhagen has already staked its claim to the North Pole, reportedly has designs on some of the islands in the Arctic Archipelago, and is aggressively pursuing exploration and discovery in its "exclusive economic zone" off Greenland, which it controls. That zone seems to expand almost yearly. Delay, however, might be in the Canadian interest if we use the time gained to improve our bargaining power by strengthening our presence in the area and in the Arctic Archipelago generally. The point is that Canada's sovereignty is not assured in the North, and the loss of Hans Island, should it occur, would be a terrible precedent—and an encouragement to other states with claims in the Arctic.

As this story suggests, Canadians' easy assumptions of sovereignty are made in ignorance, and the vast majority have never been to the Arctic. They do not realize that fewer than 120,000 people live in the Northwest Territories, Yukon, and Nunavut, or that 46 percent of Canada's territory lies north of the tree-line and is thus in the Arctic. They simply do not know that 70 percent of Canada, including the entire Arctic, has no road network and that the solitary highway into the North ends at Tuktoyaktuk on the edge of the Arctic Ocean—and this road is not all-weather. They do not understand that almost the entire Arctic Archipelago, the 19,000 islands and rocks that lie north of the mainland and are covered almost all year by ice, can be supplied only by air at present. They do not realize that, north of Baffin Island, there are only four settlements with at most eight hundred residents (including four hundred government officials) and that, on Baffin Island itself (as large as the British Isles), there are only two additional small settlements. The Arctic, in other words, is almost unpopulated, certainly undefended, and all but inaccessible to the rest of Canada.

But the Arctic is full of resources—oil, gas, minerals, gold, diamonds—and, as global warming proceeds inexorably, the control of these resources, these islands and seas, will be hotly contested. The U.S. Geological Survey estimates that a quarter of the now undiscovered oil resources will be found in the Arctic, perhaps as much as 50 billion barrels. There will also be vast quantities of natural gas. That is why the United States and Canada are squabbling over the boundary in the Beaufort Sea. As the ice melts, the frozen waters will become much more navigable than at present, and the Northwest Passage will become a shipping route for everything from oil tankers to cruise liners. The Russians, after all, sent a ship to the North Pole in 2001 without the assistance of an icebreaker. A Department of National Defence briefing paper, written in February 2006 and obtained by the *National Post*, suggests that the Northwest Passage may be open to "viable summertime commercial marine traffic by as early as 2015." The Russians are already sending cruise ships through the passage and developing their Northeast Passage, and there is talk of an "Arctic Bridge" that could link Murmansk to Churchill, Manitoba. The Arctic may be Canada's patrimony, but its future is uncertain.

The problem is that the Arctic is warming. While scientists are not unanimous in their conclusions about the rate of change, the consensus suggests that the circumpolar north is in the midst of rapid climactic change, with an estimated average rise in temperature of 5 to 7 degrees Celsius over the next century. In the summer of 2006, for example, temperatures in parts of the North were as much as 3 degrees Celsius warmer than average. Already, there is 25 percent less ice—or 2 million square kilometres—than thirty years ago, and the ice is about one-third thinner. The ice is melting at a rate of 0.7 percent a year—in normal years. In 2004–5, however, the decline (mostly in the Eastern Arctic) was a terrifying 14 percent, an area of 730,000 square kilometres. In as little as two decades, much of the Arctic Ocean may be ice free in summer. The impact of such change on the Inuit and on the fragile ecosystem—the walrus is on the verge of extinction today, and there is a northward shift of some other species into Arctic regions—is sure to be dramatic. And this impact will only be accelerated as increased shipping and resource exploration strains the regional ecology. The one possible benefit is that a reduction in the ice might open new areas to fishing. When that occurs, we will have the obligation to promulgate rules and regulations to make the fishery sustainable.

The first problem in grappling with this changing situation is the map. Most commonly, we look at Canada and the world in the Mercator projection, which puts us in the middle and stretches the rest of the world out to the east and west. (I remember how surprised I was on my first visit to Tokyo more than twenty years ago to discover that Japanese cartography put Japan in the centre of the world!) If we look at the globe from above the North Pole, however, the perspective is very different. Murmansk really is closer to Churchill if a northern route is followed. The distance from most of Asia to

Europe is some 8,000 kilometres less than the standard route through the Panama Canal. For supertankers, which now must go around Cape Horn at the bottom of South America, the voyage through the Northwest Passage might be as much as 17,000 kilometres less. Thus, change is coming. The only question is whether Canada can manage it effectively.

* * *

The image of the North in Canadian history has a way of changing dramatically from one era to the next. It is almost as if, to quote Dr. Harriet Critchley, "we have a kind of national collective schizophrenia where the Arctic is concerned." First, the North was a barren frozen waste, a land without people other than the Inuit and lost explorers. A few decades later, the Arctic became a land of opportunity and a storehouse of riches, a territory to be exploited and protected for its resources and its strategic worth. At the onset of the Cold War, the Arctic was the defence frontier against Soviet attack, the site of the Distant Early Warning Line that aimed to give the populated regions of the continent as much warning as possible before the Bear and Bison bombers destroyed Pittsburgh, New York, and Toronto with atomic bombs.

Simultaneously, the North became the locus for John Diefenbaker's "vision" for development, with Canada constructing big roads to great resources. Liberal leader Lester Pearson jeered at this notion as creating roads from igloo to igloo. Pearson was wrong to sneer (and politically foolish to do so, for Canadians loved the idea of the North), but, typically, nothing resulted from Dief's northern vision. Economic recession put paid to his sketchy plans, and military cutbacks ensured that few soldiers or airmen were ever based "north of 60." What did raise hopes was oil, the discoveries in the Beaufort Sea and the talk of pipelines through the Mackenzie Valley, but it is fair to say that, thus far, the dream of riches has yet to materialize fully. The North has always been next-year country or, perhaps, the next generation's country. Certainly it was never land Canadians were prepared to defend or exploit.

Canada acquired title to its northern lands in 1870, when the Hudson's Bay Company transferred ownership of the territory it controlled. This area was vast—Charles II had granted Rupert's Land, the watershed of Hudson Bay, to the company in 1670—and included almost half of present-day Canada. The company in 1821 subsequently acquired all the lands that make up the rest of the Northwest Territories and present-day Nunavut to the coast of the Arctic Ocean. Then, in 1880, Great Britain transferred control of the Arctic islands to the dominion, including "all Islands adjacent to such Territories."

Canada's title to the mainland is usually considered to be uncontestable, and our control over the Arctic islands is secure but not completely unchallenged. While much of the early exploration was by Britons, nationals from other countries, notably Norwegians, Danes, and Americans, made the first recorded exploration of many of the islands. There is also considerable legal doubt whether Britain could give Canada all the islands yet to be discovered.

Certainly there were continued efforts at exploration and some formal claims. The Americans explored Ellesmere Island, and Robert Peary trekked to the North Pole from there in 1909. The Norwegian Otto Sverdrup travelled widely in the Arctic Archipelago at the turn of the twentieth century, discovering and naming Axel Heiberg Island, Ellef Ringnes and Amund Rignes islands, planting his country's flag, erecting cairns, and claiming the vast territory (almost 300,000 square kilometres) for his country. The great Norwegian adventurer-explorer Roald Amundsen also worked in the Arctic, becoming the first, between 1903 and 1906, to traverse the Northwest Passage. In 1930 O.D. Skelton, the Undersecretary of State for External Affairs, negotiated a deal to extinguish Norway's claims: Canada paid Sverdrup $67,000 for his maps and records, and the next year Norway agreed not to press its claims.

What persuaded Ottawa to take the status of its claims in the Arctic seriously was, first, the Alaska Boundary Dispute with the Americans at the beginning of the twentieth century. Canada's claims were solid, but President Theodore Roosevelt was unsatisfied, and an arbitration panel, where the deciding vote was cast by a Briton, gave away much of the territory to the Americans. That concerned Ottawa, which was then also worrying about the activities of U.S. whalers on Herschel Island. As a result, the government decided to establish a North-West Mounted Police patrol there to show the flag in the western Arctic. When Denmark declared Ellesmere Island to be a no man's land in 1919, Ottawa again sent the Mounties in. By 1922 RCMP outposts had been established; others followed throughout the eastern Arctic, including the operation of a post office on Bache Island—where mail was sent and received once a year. The operation of a postal service was internationally recognized as an exercise of sovereignty.

Canada also sponsored explorations of its own. Captain J.-E. Bernier led a series of voyages in the North in the first quarter of the twentieth century. In 1909 he put a plaque in place on Melville Island, staking Canada's claim to the entire Arctic Archipelago—from the mainland to the North Pole. Vilhjalmur Stefansson, the Manitoba-born explorer, led the Canadian Arctic Expedition in 1913 that claimed the remaining western Arctic Islands for Canada. The Northern Territories Act of 1925 staked Canada's claim to the islands and waters north of the Canadian coast. The "sector theory," which saw sub-Arctic nations claim special rights in the Arctic in the polar triangle bounded by their coast and meridian lines to the North Pole, also proclaimed Canada's sovereignty.

In truth, Canadian efforts to stake its claims to the islands varied. Most of the archipelago remained uninhabited; some islands had no RCMP or government presence; and some that had once enjoyed police presence no longer did. Most seriously in doubt was Canadian control over the Northwest Passage, the ice-covered straits and channels that meandered across the top of the continent. To Canada, these were internal waters—any foreign ship wishing to use them required Ottawa's permission. To other nations, the Northwest Passage was a strait like the others, and the fact that it was effectively icebound almost all year round did not matter.

The issue of the passage came to the fore when American exploration discovered oil off Alaska. In 1969 the United States dispatched the Humble Oil Company's specially reinforced tanker, the SS *Manhattan*, through the Northwest Passage in fifteen days—by far the quickest of the sixty-nine transits since 1903—with the assistance of a Canadian icebreaker. What was lacking was Ottawa's permission, and this effrontery set off a major nationalist outcry in Canada about the fate of the North. First, the lack of permission galled Canadians, followed closely by concerns about what might happen to the fragile ecosystem of the Arctic in the event of a major oil spill. Public opinion all but forced the Trudeau government to assert jurisdiction over Canada's frozen seas, first by extending the territorial limit from 3 to 12 miles in 1970.

Then came the innovative Arctic Waters Pollution Prevention Act of the same year, which argued that the special dangers of Arctic pollution demanded Canadian control over all Arctic shipping. Canada unilaterally extended its sovereignty beyond the 12-mile limit by creating a 100-mile pollution zone. The right of commercial use was not suspended, but Ottawa redefined "innocent passage" to include environmental issues and the potential pollution threat of shipping in the Northwest Passage. Few seemed to notice that Canada had no ships capable of transiting the High Arctic to enforce the new regulations. Lest anyone—listen up, Washington!—challenge this policy, which had no standing under international law, Ottawa declared that it would not accept adjudication by the International Court of Justice in The Hague. When Washington expressed its fury, Ottawa campaigned to bring other northern nations onside, including the Soviet Union. The next time the *Manhattan* sailed, its owners accepted Canada's conditions. To bolster its claims further, Canada pressed very hard to have the 1982 United Nations Convention on the Law of the Sea include, as Article 234, the ice-covered waters clause—permission for a state to pass legislation that exceeds international standards for any ice-covered waters within its 200-mile Exclusive Economic Zone. The Arctic Waters Pollution Prevention Act thus had international sanction.

But the United States had not given up: the Americans, as a

global power, have a vital national interest in seeing their navy able to operate untrammelled through international straits. A Canadian Northwest Passage precedent might cause problems elsewhere—the Straits of Hormuz, for example. The Americans continued to send their nuclear submarines under the ice cap (as did, and do in all likelihood, the British, French, and the Soviets/Russians, too). Then, in the summer of 1985, the U.S. Coast Guard icebreaker *Polar Sea* went through the Northwest Passage from east to west without asking Canadian permission (though Canada granted permission, despite not being asked, and the vessel sailed with Canadian observers aboard). Secretary of State for External Affairs Joe Clark responded for the Mulroney government in the House of Commons on September 10, 1985, by saying that "Canada's sovereignty in the Arctic is indivisible. It embraces land, sea, and ice. It extends without interruption to the seaward-facing coasts of the Arctic Islands. These Islands are joined and not divided by the waters between them. They are bridged for most of the year by ice. From time immemorial Canada's Inuit people have used and occupied the ice as they have used and occupied the land."

Clark's statement was not enough to stop the nationalist pressure for tougher action, and the Mulroney government responded vigorously in 1986 by clarifying Canada's claims in the Arctic with the establishment of straight baselines between the outer headlands of the archipelago, rather than its previous claim that followed the shores of the islands. This move, justified on the grounds of "historic usage," made the channels within the baselines Canadian internal waters and, in effect, extended Canada's boundaries substantially. The ongoing use and occupation of the ice-covered Northwest Passage by the Inuit "from time immemorial" is another legal "hook" on which Canada hangs its claims. (The Nunavut Land Claims Agreement of 1993 reinforced the historic usage argument with its statement that "Canada's sovereignty over the waters of the Arctic archipelago is supported by Inuit use and occupancy.") However, neither the United States nor the European Union accepted Canada's claims. Ironically, it was the British, those who had ceded the Arctic Archipelago to Canada, who lodged the European Union's protest.

* * *

The Canadian military presence in the North had never been impressive. The Second World War saw the United States build the Alaska Highway and the Canol Pipeline through Canadian territory—and the Mackenzie King government paid in full for all installations after the war to ensure that Canadian sovereignty was not jeopardized. At the same time, the war put airfields and weather stations into the Arctic, an indication of the growing military importance of this area. The Cold War kept them there.

But Western Europe, not the Arctic, was Canada's focus. In the 1950s Foreign Minister Lester Pearson joked that Canada's response to a Soviet invasion of the North would be "scorched ice." In truth, Canada did not have enough troops stationed there to light a match. For a time the army had an airborne battalion based to the south and charged with opposing any lodgements in the North, and there were a few postwar exercises to test operational capabilities and equipment. Beyond a base at Churchill, Manitoba, with a small research capability, the North was as empty of Canadian forces as it had been when a few lonely Mounties lived at a handful of posts in the high Arctic to proclaim Canada's sovereignty.

The Trudeau government established a tiny northern army headquarters in 1970 and sent navy vessels north, but did little of permanence. The Mulroney government in its turn announced an increased military and naval surveillance presence (hitherto there had been only sixteen flights each year by Aurora patrol aircraft) and the construction of a very large Polar Class 8 icebreaker of 38,000 tonnes at a cost of $500 to 900 million. Significantly, Ottawa dropped its refusal to allow international courts to decide the matter of sovereignty—an expression, probably, that Ottawa believed it had mustered enough international support to prevail over any challenge.

Most important, Prime Minister Brian Mulroney raised the issue when he met President Ronald Reagan in 1986, and the dispute made its way onto the agenda when the two met again in Ottawa in April 1987 and agreed to assign resolution of the dispute to special envoys. The result, negotiated by Derek Burney for Canada, was a neighbourly solution: "I don't mind you cutting across my lawn to go to the corner store provided you ask first." The 1988 agreement, as Burney wrote in his memoirs, stipulated that "without prejudice to either side's legal position," the United States henceforth would seek permission to transit the Northwest Passage. In return, Canada undertook to grant permission. Both countries continued officially to ignore the transit of American nuclear-powered submarines through Canadian northern waters.* Still, the thorny

*Commodore (Ret'd) Eric Lerhe tells the story of a recent conference on Arctic pollution where a Canadian Coast Guard researcher talked of water samples collected from the Arctic Ocean. "So I asked her: 'Where did you get

legal issues remained unresolved, and the willingness of other nations to seek Canadian permission untested, but the irritation factor with the United States had been eliminated.

The icebreaker and the defence measures in the North promised by the government did not make it into the 1986 budget, though the promises appeared again when *Challenge and Commitment: A Defence Policy for Canada*, the 1987 White Paper on defence, reiterated and expanded them by declaring that Canada would acquire a fleet of up to twelve nuclear submarines. Atomic-powered submarines could operate under the ice cap in the Arctic, making them "the only vessel able to exercise surveillance and control in northern Canadian ice-covered waters." *Challenge and Commitment* also promised to create five forward airfields from which CF-18 fighters could operate—Yellowknife, Inuvik, Rankin Inlet, Kuujjuaq, and Iqaluit. This construction was done, and as recently as 2006 the air force held exercises at some of these airfields. The other pledges, most notably the submarines and the icebreaker, quickly dissolved into the nothingness that, historically, has so often plagued high-cost defence promises in Canada. Canada subsequently acquired used British submarines, but these conventional boats had no under-ice capability.

In fact, as the Cold War came to its end, Canada began major reductions in its (already paltry) northern military presence. In 1989 the navy ceased its annual deployments of one to three ships to the North, a practice it had followed since the Trudeau government made sovereignty a priority

those samples? And she said . . . 'From a U.S. nuclear submarine.'" In other words, U.S. submarine patrols through the Arctic are so common that they do research for Canadian scientists.

after the *Manhattan* voyage. The number of northern surveillance flights similarly was all but inconsequential, down to at most one a year by 1995—a reflection of the increasing obsolescence of the air force's Aurora aircraft and the Chrétien government's utter lack of interest in the North. The North Warning System, the modernized version of the Cold War's Distant Early Warning Line, began operating in the mid-1980s, a product of Mulroney's close relationship with President Reagan. The collapse of the Soviet Union, however, made major reductions in both personnel and radar locations possible, and some sites were automated. At roughly the same time, the Canadian Forces post at Alert, intercepting Soviet communications, was reduced in strength. As all this downsizing suggests, the greatest threat to Canada's control of its high Arctic is not the Americans or other nations, but the recent unwillingness of Canadian governments, Liberal or Conservative, to do anything to establish and sustain sovereignty and military control of the North.

Governments promised much, depending on the emphasis they gave to sovereignty, but none delivered. "We have so little capability in the North it's a national embarrassment, said Colonel Pierre Leblanc, a former commander of the Canadian Forces Northern Area. Professor Rob Huebert of the Centre for Military and Strategic Studies at the University of Calgary tells the story of a Chinese research ship arriving at Tuktoyaktuk in 1999, to the complete surprise of local officials. The Chinese had advised the Canadian Embassy in Beijing of their plans, and, if Ottawa had been told, no one had thought to tell the locals. Nor, most tellingly, did Canada's lackadaisical surveillance of its waters detect the vessel. That was likely the major piece of information the Chinese researchers took away with them.

Part of the difficulty is that Canada's main military force in the North and the Arctic was, and is, the Canadian Rangers, a force formed in 1947 "to provide a military presence in those sparsely settled northern, coastal and isolated areas of Canada which cannot conveniently or economically be provided by other components of the Canadian Forces," or so the Rangers' mandate declares. With fifty-nine patrols organized geographically, with a maximum strength of thirty, and commanded by 1 Canadian Ranger Patrol Group, there are 1,500-plus part-time Rangers (along with numbers of Junior Canadian Rangers, in effect cadets). Within three years, the intention is to reach a strength of 1,800 Rangers and 900 Junior Rangers. All Rangers have ten days of "orientation," or training; they are identifiable by their red baseball caps and sweatshirts; and they are armed with Second World War–era .303 Lee-Enfield rifles, which have the great virtue of functioning in extreme cold. They are the nation's eyes and ears in the North, and they, along with old Twin Otter aircraft and the radio intercept facility at Alert, form the front line of Canada's defence of its sovereignty.

Located in 60 communities, almost all on the mainland and not on the Arctic islands, the Rangers' task is to report unusual incidents, collect local data, help with search and rescue activities, and assist the Canadian Forces to operate in their area. The satellite telephones they would need to report intrusions quickly have never been provided—an obvious, inexpensive measure that could easily be remedied to increase the Rangers' value. In 2004 Rangers from Nunavut assisted the frigate HMCS *Montreal*, a flight of Griffon helicopters, and

160 regular force soldiers of the Royal Canadian Regiment engaged on a trouble-plagued Arctic exercise (including helicopter and snowmobile breakdowns and troops stranded by freak snowstorms). This activity was so unusual that it got major press coverage, even in the *New York Times.* The Rangers are as effective as they can be, and an inexpensive method of projecting and protecting Canadian interests. But they are also completely insufficient for the current task in the North.

* * *

Stephen Harper won the 2006 election, and his party's campaign had promised more attention to Canadian defence and the protection of sovereignty in the North. The Liberals had scoffed—Harper's plan was an expensive response to a non-existent threat, Defence Minister Bill Graham said in a curious reaction from the man who had flown to Hans Island to affirm Canada's sovereignty. But the Conservative leader had sounded determined: "As Prime Minister," he said on December 22, 2005, "I will make it plain to foreign governments—including the United States—that naval vessels travelling in Canadian waters will require the consent of the Government of Canada." Then, ten days before Harper was sworn in as Prime Minister, David Wilkins, the U.S. Ambassador to Canada, spoke at a conference at the University of Western Ontario and handed Harper an unexpected opportunity to make his point.

Wilkins reminded his audience that the United States did not recognize Canada's claim that the Northwest Passage was Canadian waters. "Our position is very consistent," he said correctly. "We agree to disagree. We don't recognize Canada's claims to the waters." There was almost no media coverage of

Wilkins's words, but at Harper's first press conference after the election, when no reporter bothered to pose a question about what the Ambassador had said, the Prime Minister–designate went out of his way to state the Canadian position: "We have significant plans for national defence and for defence of our sovereignty, including Arctic sovereignty," he said. "We believe we have the mandate for those from the Canadian people, and we hope to have it as well from the House of Commons, but it is the Canadian people we get our mandate from, not the ambassador from the United States."

To some, by leaping to slap down the American Ambassador, Harper seemed to be playing the old game: the new Tories would use anti-Americanism the same way the Grits had employed it. I believe that this assessment is wrong. Harper was, of course, making a political point. He knew Canadians worried that he was Dubya's lapdog, far too friendly to the United States. What better way to indicate he was not an American patsy than to pick up on the anodyne comments by the Ambassador about the U.S. position on Arctic waters? Quick as a flash, by slapping down Wilkins, Harper demonstrated that he was Canadian first.

Nor was this response the mindless anti-Americanism of the "Bush is a moron" type that marked the Chrétien-Martin era. Harper's was the correct kind of pro-Canadian comment. The North is ours, and we have the political will to ensure that it remains so, Harper meant. To the new Prime Minister, to whom Canadian-American cooperation in North America and the world obviously matters, Canada is nonetheless a different nation with its own national interests. On most issues of the early twenty-first century, Canada and the United States will agree because their interests and values mesh. But on some, Canadian national interests will differ, and there, Harper said, the Government of Canada will stand firm. Moreover, by speaking out for Canadian sovereignty over the Arctic, Harper picked up on one of the themes of his election campaign: a greater military emphasis in the North. Canada's North has only 150 regulars stationed at Joint Task Force North in Yellowknife, and a small air squadron with some fifty-five aircrew and support staff. The Tory campaign pledged to do much more.

First, the Conservatives stated they would build three large armed icebreakers, capable of carrying some troops, and to station them at a new all-year military-civil deep-water docking Arctic port, likely at or near Iqaluit on Baffin Island. By the spring of 2006, however, Defence Minister Gordon O'Connor had begun backing away from the icebreaker pledge. The navy suggested that other ships might be more useful—notably, four to six corvettes based on the Norwegian *Svalbard* design, armed with a 57 mm gun and missiles, and equipped with a helicopter pad, at some $250 million each. The corvettes, which might be crewed by naval reservists in a homeland defence role, certainly would be an improvement on the navy's present capabilities (and they have the additional advantage of being double the size of the Danes' Thetis-class ships), but they would not be able to sail into ice thicker than 1 metre: "They are not going to be able to get into areas with multi-year ice," said northern expert Rob Huebert.

The outcome of this Defence Department dispute remains uncertain, but the Minister is said to be determined to have strategy and capabilities in place to meet the nation's anticipated Arctic needs for the next decade. New icebreakers with the ability to operate in multi-year ice are needed to show the flag, an important task in asserting sovereignty, as well as to break ice—whether the navy or the Canadian Coast Guard operates them. The navy and the Senate's National Security and Defence Committee believe the Coast Guard should operate the icebreakers, as it has been doing for decades, and naval experts agree that "red-hulled" Coast Guard ships suggest, by their presence, civilian control of Canada's internal waters; "grey-hulled" navy ships imply that the passage is high seas or international.* The Coast Guard's one heavy icebreaker, *Louis St. Laurent*, is due for retirement in 2009, and three of the remaining four icebreakers should be replaced around the time the Tories' three new breakers, if built, would come into service. The one certainty is that Canada will need icebreakers, sooner rather than later and in larger numbers. Moreover, the government sensibly declared that all future naval construction will be capable of operating in limited ice conditions.

The Conservatives also promised to construct an Arctic National Sensor System to detect submarines and other vessels travelling in northern waters. They pledged to create an army emergency response battalion with airlift and to operate a winter warfare training school near Cambridge Bay; to increase air patrols; and, in order to provide continuous surveillance, to station long-range Uninhabited Aerial Vehicles (UAVs) at Goose Bay in Labrador and at Comox in British Columbia. The Tories also stated that, by stationing new fixed-wing search

*Peter Haydon, a retired naval officer and naval scholar, suggests that the navy might take operational control of Coast Guard heavy icebreakers in the Arctic "so that an effective air and surface Arctic patrol regime can be established."

and rescue aircraft at Yellowknife, they would improve search and rescue capabilities for the inevitable day when a large passenger aircraft crashed in the North.* All these measures are expensive, certainly more than the $2 billion the Conservatives estimated, but, if implemented, they will be hugely important in establishing the strength of Canada's claims in the Far North. With *RadarSat-2*, a space satellite approved by the Liberal government and scheduled for launch in March 2007, Canada will acquire the capacity to observe all surface vessels in Canadian Arctic waters twenty-four hours a day. Its impact on the government's ability to gather information will be great.

An Arctic port, estimated to cost at least $200 million to construct and equip, has additional benefits. It could dramatically reduce the high cost of living in the Far North by opening the Arctic to regular resupply by ship, and it could provide that rarest of northern attributes—good jobs for port workers and for those who could provide tourist facilities for cruise ships and support for fishing vessels.† A port will spur the search for and development of oil, gas, minerals, and diamonds, and all

*The short-lived Martin government had shown more interest in "putting footprints in the snow" than its immediate predecessor, and its Defence Policy Statement in 2005 did call for increased surveillance in the North by upgraded Auroras, testing Unmanned Aerial Vehicles on Baffin Island, and "Project Polar Epsilon," a plan to piggyback Arctic surveillance on a commercial satellite system. The Tory plan was much more extensive.

†A federal government report released in September 2006 recommended the creation of seven small ports along the Arctic coast, though no money has yet been allocated for them. "Canadian sovereignty in the North would be boosted significantly by the regular use of Nunavut harbours by federal research and patrol vessels," the report says. These ports would be in addition to the large port pledged by the Conservatives.

that activity will require infrastructure on shore. A new port, moreover, will increase ship traffic. That fact alone demands that the government implement its other measures for defending sovereignty; a new harbour without these measures will, paradoxically, weaken Canadian claims.

The test is what Canada will do with its new military capacities when—if—they come on stream.* The United States Arctic Research Commission has published a fictional "vignette" of a naval operation that might be mounted in an ice-free Arctic. In it, three U.S. Navy warships and a nuclear submarine are sent through the Northern Sea Route, the Russian equivalent of Canada's Northwest Passage, to show the flag and head off the European Union's imminent concession of transit control to Russia. The vignette does not hazard a guess as to Russia's response. That such a scenario could be published illustrates just how seriously the United States takes its position on the international character of straits such as those claimed by Canada and Russia. The U.S. National Research Council in 2006 added its voice, urging the construction of two big icebreakers "to protect not only [the United States'] territorial interests, but also its presence as a world power." The United States, the report added, needs "to assert a more active and influential presence in the Arctic."

*The Canadian navy has expressed little interest in expanding its role in the Arctic, or so "Arctic Maritime Security and Defence," a paper produced in 2005 by the Strategic Analysis Research Team in the office of the Director of Maritime Strategy at National Defence Headquarters, suggests. The broad conclusion of the study was that, notwithstanding the melting of the ice cap, the navy will have no significant role in the North in the next twenty-five years. Whether the Conservative government's desire to enhance sovereignty and to acquire armed icebreakers will change this attitude is unclear as yet.

On the other hand, Paul Cellucci, the former United States Ambassador to Canada, told a conference in Ottawa in late 2006 that if Canada controlled the Northwest Passage, this would serve U.S. security interests. Canada could police the Arctic more effectively than the United States and thus make a real contribution to North American security. There are some additional bureaucratic indications that the United States is rethinking its historic objections to Canada's claims of Arctic sovereignty. While Cellucci's successor in Ottawa, David Wilkins, promptly denied that American policy had changed, the Ambassador appeared to be scrambling. Obviously, the argument that Canada can protect North American security by taking on the task of securing the Northwest Passage is one that should be made forcefully to the Pentagon and the Administration. That this will strengthen our claims to the Passage and serve our historic national interests is the icing on the Arctic cake.

We know that Canada has no intention of sinking American or Russian or British submarines under the ice; nor will we go to war with Denmark for Hans Island unless the usually placid Danes turn into Vikings and go berserk. But simply by being there, by knowing what is happening, and by having an armed Canadian presence on hand, Canada's position will be strengthened immeasurably. Defence Minister O'Connor said in Iqaluit in July 2006: "I want the navy, the army and air force operating up here so that our airspace, our waters and our land are all under the control of Canadians, so there's no question that if people went through our land, air or water they follow our laws." That, he said, is "all part of sovereignty." "We will never refuse anybody" innocent passage, O'Connor said later, "but they've got to follow our laws." Occupation and use—the key elements in the definition of sovereignty—will be substantially increased if the Harper government follows through with its announced plans.

In April 2006, as a first measure, five patrols of the Canadian Rangers, completing a 4,500-kilometre journey, met on Lougheed Island and hammered a plaque into the frozen ground, proclaiming the territory as Canada's. At the same time, Ottawa and Copenhagen began a joint survey of an underwater mountain ridge located north of Greenland and east of Ellesmere Island. Both countries have legal claims to the continental shelf, and, despite their dispute over Hans Island, they agreed to the mapping of the Lomonosov Ridge. If the ridge is continuous, the UN Convention on the Law of the Sea specifies, Canada and Denmark can measure their claims from the outer edge—the western edge for Canada, the eastern for Denmark. The Russians have claims as well, overlapping those of the Danes and Canadians. If the survey supports the existence of a continuous shelf, Canada could claim an area as big in size as Alberta, and the Danish gain might be three times the size of Denmark. The petroleum and mineral resources in the area could be huge. It is worth noting that while Canada ratified the UN Convention in 2003, the United States has not accepted it.

In August 2006, in another Canadian sovereignty measure, one of the largest military exercises in the Arctic took place. The frigate HMCS *Montreal;* two *Kingston*-class Maritime Coastal Defence Vessels, *Moncton* and *Goose Bay;* six aircraft; and a platoon of infantry all operated in and around Baffin Island. The ships, with their moderate capability in light ice, entered Lancaster Sound, the first Canadian naval vessels to do so in three decades, and the troops, cooperating with Ranger patrols from Nunavut communities, carried out training exercises. In an appropriate touch, the group visited RCMP graves from the 1920s—the new sovereignty patrols paying respect to the remains of the old. Several cruise ships had stopped by the gravesites the week before—an indication of the Arctic shipping traffic to come.

As the ice melts, as resources become accessible, and as shipping inevitably increases, Canadian sovereignty will be tested as never before. The Arctic might be "the next Alberta," and already mineral exploration is well advanced on some of the Arctic islands. Nations will not hesitate to press their claims if the rewards seem high enough—and they do. One energy analyst, Christopher Weafer in the *New York Times*, talked of the coming tussle as the "Great Game in a cold climate," a reference to the Anglo-Russian contest for the Indian frontier in Rudyard Kipling's time. Being prepared for this coming struggle makes sense in national terms. To his great credit, Harper seems to understand the importance of the Arctic and seems willing—at least at the beginning of his mandate—to back up his words with dollars, soldiers, and equipment. Anti-Americanism in defence of Canada's national interests is the only justifiable use of this all-too-familiar toxic brew.

Beyond making the Canadian Forces able to operate in and watch over the North, many more initiatives could be undertaken. Canada has supported the legitimacy of commercial shipping in the Arctic, but the requirement remains for an enforceable compulsory regulatory regime. While the 1970 Arctic Waters Pollution Prevention Act was a good first step,

Canada had for all practical purposes no way of enforcing its terms—a grave national weakness in 1970 and even more so four decades later. Canada needs to design, put in place, and enforce a mandatory system of tough environmental controls on shipping, mining, and exploration through the Arctic waters it claims. There will be protests if Canada acts, and strong political leadership will be needed, as well as the necessary strength to enforce Canadian policy. Another essential step is to require vessels using northern waters to register with the Canadian Coast Guard's NORDREG system. Most ships do so voluntarily, to facilitate rescue should that be necessary, but those intending illegal acts, such as smuggling, or fearing that their vessels might not meet pollution standards would, presumably, not register. Compulsory registration will let Canada act against violators and, as well, strengthen Canada's claims to sovereignty.

At the same time, the Harper government needs to carry out the military promises it has made. Canada will then know what is happening in the Arctic, and Ottawa can move to get what it wants—to protect and advance the Canadian national interest in the North. On his extraordinary six-day visit to the Arctic in August 2006, the Prime Minister observed that "the economics and strategic value of northern resource development are growing more attractive and critical to our nation. And trust me," he continued, "it's not only Canadians who are noticing. It's no exaggeration to say that the need to assert our sovereignty and take action to protect our territorial integrity in the Arctic has never been more urgent." He added: "We always need to know who is in our waters and why they are there. We must be certain that everyone who enters our waters respects our laws and regulations, particularly those that protect the fragile Arctic environment." This government views the issue in its proper light.

It seems very clear to me that we cannot win a legal and political battle with the United States, Denmark, or Russia in the Arctic—except with the exertion of sustained political will. That requires the allocation of resources; in essence, we can have all the sovereignty we are willing to pay for. The demonstration of will by the Harper government to date has been impressive, but it must follow through on its promises. Thus far, the auguries are positive, and the chances of this nation retaining the fullest possible rights to all its Arctic territories seem better than they did five, ten, or twenty years ago. Harper's successors will need to be ready to exert the same political will all through this century.

It comes down to one issue, Stephen Harper said during the 2005–6 election campaign: "Sovereignty is something that you use it, or you lose it." Precisely correct, and the ball is in the Harper government's court. Canada's control of the Arctic Archipelago and the Northwest Passage is a peculiarly Canadian battle, and it is one war that the Canada of the future simply cannot afford to lose. Any government that tamely surrenders Canada's claims will never be forgiven by the Canadian people.

[6]

A Pacifist Quebec

André Boisclair was chosen to be leader of the Parti Québécois in November 2005. Young, good-looking, and articulate, he and his lifestyle seem to many observers to embody the ethos of the young professionals who now drive Quebec society. But in his policy views, Boisclair harks back to older traditions. He is, of course, a hard-line sovereignist, calling for Quebec's independence. Perhaps more surprising to some English-speaking Canadians, he proudly proclaims himself and his party as pacifist. "We are a peaceful people," he told a meeting of his party's constituency presidents in March 2006. As an independent nation with its place in the United Nations, Quebec would be "ecologist, pacifist, expressing solidarity, and favouring an alternative vision of globalization." His enthused audience responded with cheers and chants of "Un Québec pour le monde," Quebec for the world.

A pacifist Quebec? Boisclair is not the only separatist to

argue this position.* In Parliament, the Bloc Québécois defence critic, the knowledgeable André Bachand from Saint-Jean (a riding with substantial military installations), has repeatedly proclaimed that "it is true that Quebecers are pacifists." As he said in May 2003, "It is a choice that was made by Quebec society." The next year, in October, Bachand said in the House of Commons that, "in Quebec, we come from a pacifist country . . . a peace-loving country. Had it not been for us—and I say so in all modesty—I think Canada would have participated in the war in Iraq . . . I find that Quebecers were right to say no to the war. They are traditional and pacifists . . . We are soon going to be very proud, as Quebecers, to have an army that is much more peace-minded than militaristic." In September 2006, after five Canadians died in two days of fighting in Afghanistan, Bloc leader Gilles Duceppe said he believed Prime Minister Stephen Harper was "taking the same alignment" as President George Bush and, he stated, Quebecers "are firmly against that." The Tories, he added, have left behind the country's historical position of "balance and mediation" and "the major values of the Québécois," which were "resolutely peaceful."

Bachand and Duceppe were simply reiterating the present sovereignist position. In November 2004 the Bloc declared that its priority was United Nations peacekeeping, which it viewed as a fundamental role, indeed the primary role, for the Canadian Forces. Combat missions did not seem to be

*Solidarité Québec, a new left-wing separatist party in Quebec, also proclaims itself to be pacifist.

required—if NATO and NORAD were reconfigured "so that their strategic missions reflect the UN's needs."*

This talk was utter utopian pacifistic nonsense, and it reflected the fact that the separatist position on defence had been softening since the time of René Lévesque, the Parti Québécois founder and, in 1976, first premier. At that time the pledge had been offered that an independent Quebec would remain part of the North Atlantic Treaty Organization and the North American Air Defence Agreement, then effectively functioning as instruments of Cold War defence and foreign policy. This commitment essentially remained the policy through the 1995 referendum on independence, when Quebec sovereignists stated that their independent nation would have its own army, remain in Canada's alliances, engage in peacekeeping operations, and remain a defence partner with the United States and presumably Canada. The Parti Québécois draft legislation on sovereignty, as reported to Washington by the U.S. Consulate General in Quebec City before the referendum, stated that an independent Quebec "will maintain forces proportional to its size and needs . . . and will assume responsibilities in collective security and defence."

Bloc Québécois leader Lucien Bouchard had said much the same in Parliament in March 1994: "Canada has been a faithful

*A survey by the Canadian Forces, "Canada's Soldiers: Military Ethos and Canadian Values in the 21st Century," released in March 2005, found that Quebec-based soldiers, the great majority of whom are French-speaking, have "a completely different view" from other Canadian soldiers on their roles, most preferring "non-combat operations in Canada." Anglophone soldiers saw combat to defend Canada and combat abroad as their preferred roles. Another DND survey found that 62 percent of Quebecers favoured "traditional peacekeeping roles."

ally of the U.S. The same will be true of a sovereign Quebec. Whatever happens overseas, we will continue to share a common geo-political space and to contribute to its defence . . . I understand that certain countries did not have the choice of being neutral or not being neutral," Bouchard said. "But neutralism is not my cup of tea. Neutralism did not win the Cold War. And this kind of neutralism which is made of indifference and passivity will not win the peace in the hot spots of the world." But Bouchard is now gone from the councils of the separatists, and so too, it seems, is his anti-neutralist and anti-pacifist voice.

Bouchard's support for alliances and against neutralism/pacifism sounded genuine, but it was likely also tactical and practical politics. First there were thousands of Québécois who had served and were serving in the Canadian Forces. They were voters, and they might be expected to be concerned with the defence policy of the new Quebec and with their jobs. (During the 1995 referendum, the "Oui" campaign invited Canadian Forces members to join the Quebec military after a successful secession.) Moreover, reassuring the United States, the superpower next door, that little would change if Quebec became independent was smart politics.

If that was the tactic, it did not succeed. Quebec Deputy Premier Bernard Landry wrote to U.S. Secretary of State Warren Christopher in October 1995 to urge Washington to stay out of the 1995 referendum campaign. With Landry's usual ham-handedness, he stupidly threatened that, "should American declarations be publicly perceived as a factor in the decision that Quebecers are to make, they would enter into our collective memory . . . If victory eludes the Yes side by a slim margin, as is plausible, those who did vote Yes—a clear majority of francophone Quebecers—will be tempted to assign responsibility to the United States." The letter inevitably leaked to the media, and it virtually forced the United States to take a position. Both President Bill Clinton and his Secretary of State duly spoke out for a united Canada in the 1995 referendum campaign. Clinton said that a united Canada had been "a strong and powerful ally of ours. And I have to tell you that I hope that will continue . . . Now the people of Quebec will have to cast their votes as their lights guide them," the President went on. "But Canada has been a great model for the rest of the world . . . and I hope that can continue." Clinton's intervention might well have tipped the balance against the "Oui" in that very close contest with the "Non," when it won by only 1.2 percent, or 50,498 votes.

Why was the United States in favour of seeing Canada stay intact? There are many reasons, ranging from preferring to deal with one nation to its north to concerns over the defence of North America. Dwight Mason, a long-time senior diplomat in the American Embassy in Ottawa and a former chair of the U.S. Section of the Permanent Joint Board on Defense, wrote sharply in January 2006 of the 1995 referendum that "Quebec independence would greatly complicate and perhaps unravel existing North American economic, defense, and other relationships which are in the United States best interests to preserve and strengthen." At the minimum, Mason said, Quebec independence would have resulted in a troubled transition in which North American relationships would have been in disarray. There is absolutely no reason to believe that the American position will be any different in a subsequent referendum on independence. Indeed, after the attacks of September 11, and with the tide of anti-Americanism* and pacifism currently at full flood in Quebec, the American hostility to independence for Quebec can be expected to be even sharper. I would suggest that, today, the main factor in the U.S. position will be security and the probability, in American eyes, that a sovereign Quebec will not do much, if anything, for North American defence. Americans will likely look at the historical record in the province and the pacifist attitudes expressed today, and they will not be amused.

* * *

Quebec was not always pacifist and neutralist. New France had been a military society, one that waged war against the natives and the English settlers to their south with bloody ferocity. Some Québécois had battled against the American invaders in 1775, and more had done so during the War of 1812. The militia tradition in Lower Canada was strong, and it remained viable after Confederation. What sapped the military fervour of Quebec was a succession of crises that seemed all but irrelevant to francophones. The first was the 1885 Riel Rebellion in the North-West. Initially, Quebec militia had been keen to serve, but the execution of Riel and the glee with which the English-speaking greeted his hanging eliminated any enthusiasm. The

*A poll conducted for the Association for Canadian Studies in September 2006 by Léger found that 77 percent of Quebecers agreed that September 11 was the result of U.S. policy. Even former PQ premier Lucien Bouchard bemoaned the rising anti-American tide in October 2006: "It is where we export 85 percent of what we produce. They ensure our continental defence. We cannot judge Americans like that because of the current situation."

South African War a decade and a half later saw imperialist fervour in Ontario and the West, but only resentment in Quebec that Britain and a few English-language newspapers had hustled Canada into a war against the Boers, a people much like the Québécois themselves. And the debate over the provision of dreadnaughts for the Royal Navy in 1912 again drew no support from francophones.

Thus, by the time of the Great War, Quebec had become an anti-military society or, to put it more exactly, a society against participation in British wars. In August 1914 anglophones hurried to enlist in Montreal, the Eastern Townships, and Quebec City, but the French-speaking hung back. There were 1,200 in the first contingent to go overseas in the autumn of 1914, but, by the time of Vimy Ridge in April 1917, the Canadian Corps of four divisions with forty-eight infantry battalions contained only one French-speaking battalion, the 22e Régiment. It is impossible to calculate precisely the number of francophones who volunteered for the front, but the low estimate is around 12,000 and the high, perhaps 25,000. Even counting conscripts, called to service after the election of December 1917 (which was won by Sir Robert Borden and his Unionist Government running flat out against Quebec), the total of francophone enlistment (which includes the French-speaking from other provinces) was at most 50,000, or roughly one in thirteen of those enlisted in the Canadian Expeditionary Force.

Given that the francophone population of Canada at the time was close to 35 percent, the disparity was marked. Worse, Anglo-Canadians noticed and commented on French Canada's low enlistment record. Quebec had failed to do its duty in the war, Winnipeg publisher John W. Dafoe wrote to a French-speaking friend, "the only known race of white men to quit." Dafoe was ordinarily a balanced, fair man, and his brutal words were an indicator of how strong the feeling had become. Quebecers responded that if English Canadians didn't want them in Canada, they were prepared to consider leaving Confederation.

The postwar reaction all across the nation was to put the war into the past. Government policy tried to reassure Quebec that Canada would not go to war again and, if it ever did, there would never be conscription. Both promises turned out to be false.

When Mackenzie King took Canada to war against Hitler in September 1939, he did so on the promise, first, that it would be a war of limited liability—no big armies and a minimal expenditure of blood and treasure. That promise disappeared into the ether after the fall of France in June 1940, when Britain found itself alone and in grave danger of defeat. So too did the promises of no conscription. In June 1940 Parliament passed the National Resources Mobilization Act, a home defence conscription measure. In April 1942 the country—except for Quebec, francophones outside Quebec, and some ethnic Ukrainian and German constituencies—voted heavily for the implementation of overseas conscription. And in November 1944, when infantry casualties at the front outstripped the reinforcement system, Mackenzie King finally ordered 16,000 home defence conscripts overseas. At each step along the way, an outraged Quebec argued that the promises made to it, and it alone, had been broken. Perhaps 150,000 francophones volunteered or were conscripted in the Second World War out of a Canadian total of 1.1 million men and women in uniform, and many French Canadians were among Canada's most decorated and effective soldiers. Nonetheless, according to historian Béatrice Richard, only some 84,000 to 90,000 came from Quebec, or, at most, 8 percent of total Canadian enlistment. The total francophone enlistment, however, was almost double the percentage in the Great War. That Canada's national interests had been threatened, that merchant and naval ships had been sunk by U-boats in the Gulf of St. Lawrence, and that the bodies of seamen had washed up on the Gaspé shores may have had something to do with the higher enlistments.

What was striking, all the same, was how Quebec's elites and intellectuals viewed the conflict. To young men like Pierre Elliott Trudeau, twenty years old when the war began, the conflict was of little interest. Canada was not threatened, the fate of France was all but inconsequential, and, while Hitler was evil, Quebec should sit out the fighting and oppose conscription, though it would take any war factories that might be offered. To read Trudeau's wartime writings, to peruse the pro-Vichy wartime editorial pages of *Le Devoir*, to go over the *nationaliste* speeches against conscription and against Charles de Gaulle's Free France is to believe that a severe form of blindness afflicted the intellectual leaders of French Canada. As Trudeau's very able official biographer, John English, notes matter-of-factly, only one of the forty graduates in Trudeau's 1939–40 class at Collège Jean-de-Brébeuf went into the armed forces. The results in any comparable graduating class elsewhere in Canada were very different. Still, that so many ordinary francophones enlisted despite the near unanimity of their leaders' anti-war opinions was a miracle. Trudeau himself began to realize that the war was about freedom and the survival of democracy only when he went to Harvard University in 1944, read about Nazism, and saw that the United States was wholeheartedly in the conflict. It was not just a British war after all.

In the immediate postwar years, Canada disarmed as quickly as it could, implicitly pleading for the world to leave it alone. But the Soviet Union was aggressive, and Communist parties in Western Europe posed a new threat to the democracies. The result in 1949 was the signing of the North Atlantic Treaty, with Canada as one of its key originators. The Secretary of State for External Affairs at the time the treaty was negotiated was Louis St. Laurent; by the time it was signed, he was Prime Minister.

A Quebec City corporate lawyer, St. Laurent had joined Mackenzie King's wartime government as Justice Minister in late 1941. He supported conscription in November 1944 because he believed it to be the only way to get the reinforcements the First Canadian Army fighting in Northwest Europe and Italy required. He then won the leadership of the Liberal Party in convention and became Prime Minister in the fall of 1948. He took Canada into NATO, the nation's first peacetime military alliance, and won a smashing victory in the election of 1949. In Quebec his Liberals took sixty-eight of seventy-three seats. The next year, war broke out in Korea in June 1950, and St. Laurent committed the country to the United Nations "police action," sending ships, aircraft, and an infantry brigade to fight against North Korean and Communist Chinese troops. There were no huzzas from the Québécois, as always against participation in war anywhere, but neither were there demonstrations in the street.

Soon after going into Korea, St. Laurent sent an air division of fighter aircraft and a brigade group of infantry to Germany as part of Canada's commitment to NATO; at the same time, the navy began its expansion into a major fleet in the North Atlantic. His government poured huge sums into rearmament, the military rising in strength towards 120,000 men, while defence spending crested at over 7 percent of gross domestic product. (The current figure is around 1.2 percent of GDP.) Again, no one cheered in Quebec, and opposition to the Liberal government's defence policy increased. In the 1953 election, however, St. Laurent's Liberals won sixty-six of seventy-five seats and another big majority. Even in 1957, the election St. Laurent narrowly lost to John Diefenbaker, he held on to the party's Quebec base, taking sixty-two of seventy-five ridings.

How did St. Laurent hold Quebec support while he led Canada into the world? First, he was a very good politician, much underrated by historians. "Uncle Louis" could kiss babies with the best of them, but he was also highly intelligent, arguably the equal of Pierre Trudeau or Stephen Harper in brainpower. He thought in terms of Canada's national interests, understood the threat Soviet Communism posed to democracy, and recognized that Korea was as much a front in the Cold War as Western Europe. He knew Canada had to cooperate with the United States at home, in Europe, and in Korea. If war with the Soviets had erupted, he intended to implement conscription. Indeed, his government had already printed up the registration cards for national service.

But St. Laurent was a francophone and, having lived through the First and the Second World War, he understood that Quebec's thinking about an activist foreign and defence policy still lagged behind the rest of Canada. Opinion polls throughout the war and the postwar years made this disparity clear. What to do? First, even though memories of the 1942 and 1944 conscription crises were fresh and pacifist sentiment remained powerful, he went regularly into Quebec and spoke about the need for Canada to work with its allies—the British, the Americans, and the Western Europeans. In one speech at a service club in Saint-Jean, he pointed to a bishop at his table and, referring to how the Soviets had imprisoned the Hungarian Cardinal Mindszenty, said he did not want to see that happen in Quebec. Such very political (but truthful) messaging resonated in a still deeply Roman Catholic and anti-Communist Quebec.

At the same time, the Liberals saw to it that the province received its full share of military bases and defence contracts. Although the Canadian Army had some difficulty in recruiting enough men to keep the three battalions of the Royal 22e Régiment up to strength during the Korean fighting, St. Laurent ensured that there was no criticism of these shortfalls in government, the media, or the military. "With this prime minister," Defence Minister Brooke Claxton said early in the Korean War, "we can do anything in Quebec." That may not have been completely correct, but it was true enough that Canada—for the first time in its history—had an activist, engaged foreign policy without tearing the nation's unity to shreds.

There was an implicit bargain in place there, a concordat between Prime Minister St. Laurent and Quebec, which allowed this foreign and defence policy to move forward. We don't like the military build-up, Quebec said, but we trust this Prime Minister to do nothing rash and to see that Quebec's needs are met. We would prefer not to be in alliances overseas, but we trust St. Laurent to ensure that Canada does nothing to threaten French Canada's way of life and beliefs. Three successive Liberal sweeps in federal elections in Quebec showed the strength of the bargain. So powerful was the concordat that it lasted for a decade after St. Laurent had suffered defeat in 1957.

Matters began to change in 1968 when Pierre Elliott Trudeau became Prime Minister. He was not the young *nationaliste* of the Second World War years, and certainly his attitudes on federalism had altered completely. But in his views on war and the military, on alliances and defence, he remained very much the same man. Trudeau disliked soldiers and felt that anyone serving in the Canadian Forces was almost by definition unintelligent. He mistrusted Canada's alliances and thought they drove Canadian foreign and defence policy, rather than policy shaping Canada's alliances. In his first year in power, he almost succeeded in pulling all Canadian troops out of NATO Europe; as it was, he cut the commitment by half. He scarcely blinked when the Soviets crushed the Prague Spring and burgeoning Czechoslovakian democracy in 1968; he fought with Canada's allies; and he launched a quixotic peace mission at the end of his political career at the precise time the Soviet Union was rattling its nuclear sabres. In these ways, Trudeau, the youth, remained very similar to Trudeau, the Prime Minister.

* * *

We can, I believe, generalize from this story. If Anglo-Canadians had shaped foreign and defence policy in the world wars, French-speaking Canadians have very largely shaped it since 1968. There is no doubt—according to decades of opinion polls—that Quebec's attitudes to the military and defence spending are cool; that Quebec attitudes to Canadian participation in conflict, in any conflict, are different from those of English-speaking Canadians; and that francophone attitudes to imperialism (historically British and now American) are much more antipathetic.

Moreover, opinion polls demonstrate consistently that a deeply pacifist and anti-military Quebec is the least supportive region of the country when it comes to the government taking steps to fix the Canadian Forces. An Ipsos-Reid opinion poll in February 2003 found that only 3 percent of francophones considered military spending to be a high priority. A Compas poll in February 2005 found that one in three Québécois believed Canada should have no Canadian Forces at all. Quebec opinion used to be isolationist, but it is not any longer. It favours trade, generally looks positively on aid, and mostly supports benign blue-beret peacekeeping. Quebec was also grateful to the military during the Oka crisis in the early 1990s and after the ice storm. But francophones are persistently cold to more spending on the Canadian Forces except for traditional UN peacekeeping operations.

Canada has had a run of long-lived prime ministers from Quebec—Pierre Trudeau, Brian Mulroney, and Jean Chrétien—who, from 1968 to 2003, have been exquisitely cognizant of Quebec's attitudes and beliefs. Of course, they have all been fully aware of the strength of independentist attitudes in the province, ebbing and rising with events and the years. The result, I believe, is that Quebec drove policy in these years. If, as I will argue in the next chapter, it is bad policy to let Canadian Jews or Canadian Muslims have undue influence on Canada's policy to Israel, for example, it is similarly bad policy to let French Canada determine Canadian foreign and defence policy.

I don't believe it is too strong to say that Quebec has determined our policy. There are many examples, but let me cite just two recent events. The first was the decision to stay out of the Iraq War in 2003. It was shaped by the overwhelmingly negative attitudes in polls in Quebec and by the coincidence of the Quebec provincial election, where all three party leaders wore anti-war ribbons during the leaders' debate on TV. With the Chrétien Liberals in power in Ottawa, with the chance to see Jean Charest's Liberals defeat the Parti Québécois, Canada's decision appeared made for it. Certainly it helped that the federal Liberal women's caucus was opposed to war against Saddam Hussein and that nationalist and anti-American English-Canadian Liberals in the Cabinet, caucus, and country were vociferously opposed. Although the positions of the three opposition groups were important, the key was Quebec's vehement anti-war opinion—which Prime Minister Jean Chrétien apparently shared.*

The second example was the overwhelmingly hostile Quebec poll numbers that drove the decision to refuse to join the United States in Ballistic Missile Defence in 2005. In a minority Parliament with another election in the offing, this issue mattered. Enmeshed in the sponsorship scandal, Prime Minister Paul Martin's Liberals could not afford to upset their Quebec supporters, dwindling day by day, by agreeing to support BMD. It didn't matter that the United States asked nothing

*For a very different interpretation of this decision, see the book by Chrétien's key aide, Eddie Goldenberg, *The Way It Works* (2006): "There had never been any reference to Quebec in any of the discussions on Iraq in Cabinet or in any of my talks with the prime minister."

of Canada, neither money nor territory. Quebec opposed the idea, and that was sufficient. That the same anti-American, anti–Iraq War groups in the Liberal caucus and party opposed the deal was a bonus, but Quebec again was the key.

As I indicated earlier, I was in favour of Canada supporting the United States in Iraq and joining in Ballistic Missile Defence. My reasons were based on our national interests. Canada's economy depends on trade with the United States, and this dependence cannot be changed. We are extremely vulnerable if the administration in Washington is unhappy with us, and we are in peril if border crossings are slowed for even a few minutes more for each truck or if passports are required to cross the border. The need to keep the economy strong ought to have determined the Iraq question for us. The Ballistic Missile Defence decision was an even greater mistake in national interest terms, as Prime Minister Paul Martin abandoned any say in continental defence for the sake of a presumed transitory political advantage. That advantage turned to dust, and Martin merited his fate of being consigned to history's ashcan. With North Korea now testing nuclear weapons, with Iran on the verge of acquiring them, and with both developing longer-range missiles, the Ballistic Missile Defence decision looks more foolish every day.

* * *

But the requirement to keep Canada united is also a national interest. There is a conundrum here, and there is no doubt that, initially, on both issues, Quebec was of a very different mind from English Canada. Professor David Haglund of Queen's University described Quebec opinion on Ballistic Missile Defence as "unanimity, with near total agreement that missile defence must be bad." Opinion on the Iraq War at one point in Quebec was almost 30 percent more against Canadian participation than in Alberta, a gap of historic proportions. The key point, however, is that in neither case was there any leadership from Prime Ministers Chrétien or Martin to try to persuade Quebecers that the state of their province's economy, their jobs, and their pocketbooks might actually matter more to them than whether Canada supported the United States politically on Iraq or joined in a cost-free Ballistic Missile Defence. The latter case is strikingly clear—Martin had indicated before he wrested the prime ministership from Chrétien that he supported missile defence, but once he saw the poll numbers, once the New Democratic Party and some in the Liberal caucus began opposing it in a minority Parliament, he turned away.* An utter and complete lack of leadership decided the missile defence issue.

Despite the Chrétien-Martin examples, I continue to believe that leadership actually can be exercised by politicians on sensitive foreign policy issues. Louis St. Laurent did so. He led. He didn't shape policy by poring over tea leaves or by perusing the opinion polls. He explained why he was acting here but not there; he told the people what his policies were; and he won their acquiescence, if not the wholehearted support of everyone. That was leadership. It was also a recognition of the

*Do you think that policy decisions such as that on Ballistic Missile Defence don't affect Canada's standing in the United States? Consider this comment by David Jones, a former senior official at the U.S. Embassy in Ottawa, in the May 2005 issue of *Policy Options*: "What is essential in bilateral relationship is trust. And Prime Minister Martin has left the impression that he is not trustworthy. He cannot be relied upon—and he does not have the courage to inform directly those that he has misinformed."

country's national interests and a readiness to make sure that the people understood them and why they were so important. A prime minister needs to talk national interests to Quebec and to all Canada and to tell the same story from Montreal to Vancouver. Louis St. Laurent did. Stephen Harper and those who succeed him need to act in the same way.

* * *

I believe that anti-Americanism is a poison afflicting the Canadian body politic, an attitude that hurts the achievement of our national interests. This passion is led, currently, by francophones in Quebec. Although in 1988 Quebecers had been strongly positive about free trade (perhaps because some thought its achievement might weaken the federal state), opinion turned against it in the following few years. Quebec's historic anti-militarism and anti-imperialism began to manifest itself after the end of the Cold War, and, when George W. Bush was in the White House and taking his country into the War on Terror, Quebec anti-Americanism was the most virulent in Canada. By the time of the Iraq War in 2003, Quebec opinion was far and away the most hostile to the United States and Bush, and the province with the most anti-American attitudes in Canada. The Iraq War was a tumultuous event in Quebec, and the opposition to the war virtually total, far overshadowing that elsewhere in the country. Even if the Security Council had given the war its support, Quebec polls showed, two out of three would have opposed it—at a time when English Canada favoured a UN-sanctioned conflict by a majority of two to one. The main antiwar demonstration in Montreal, for example, saw at least 200,000 people marching in protest, compared to some

20,000 in Toronto. It was one of the largest antiwar marches in the world, and Parti Québécois Premier Bernard Landry commented: "This means that there really are two nations in Canada. Those who didn't know that can [now] see it clearly . . . this shows that Quebecers are a nation and that this nation should have international status." If, as Professor Haglund has suggested, anti-Americanism implies a willingness to think the worst of American *policy*, then it is not too difficult to establish a connection between anti-militarism and anti-Americanism. Compared with English Canadians, Québécois are, as a poll commissioned for the Canadian Defence and Foreign Affairs Institute put it, more likely nowadays to oppose the United States, to feel that they "cannot trust the United States," that "the U.S. is behaving like a rogue nation," or that "the U.S. is a force for evil in the world."

This view is most obvious when Quebec's reactions to Ballistic Missile Defence are examined. There, missile defence has at times appeared to be the most momentous issue on the policy agenda. Debate, wrote David Haglund, "is probably the wrong word to apply to the Quebec discussion of missile defence, because a proper debate presupposes that there are two sides in contention over a matter. What is noteworthy is the unanimity on display in the Quebec discussions, with near-total agreement that missile defence must be bad, the only items of disagreement arising over exactly *why* this should be so." Some in Quebec feared that missile defence would lead to a global arms race and imperil world peace. "Others worried that missile defence would have sinister implications for American foreign policy, allowing Washington to go off on a global campaign of conquest." Quebec's opposition to BMD seemed to spring from a combination of pacifism, anti-militarism, and anti-Americanism. What was most notable, indeed extraordinary, was that no one in the federal government tried to point out to Québécois why participation in this defence might be in the Canadian interest. Nor did any federal leaders indicate the risks to Canadian national interests if it was not accepted. The debate was left to the tiny cadre of francophone defence experts* and a few editorialists, and there was zero political leadership from the Prime Minister or his Quebec ministers. Zero. The failure to lead was complete, and in the circumstances the state of francophone public opinion was completely predictable.

Quebec's opposition to the Harper government's policy in the Israeli-Hezbollah war in Lebanon in July and August 2006 seemed motivated by the same attitudes. One large "peace" parade in Montreal saw André Boisclair, Gilles Duceppe, Liberal MP Denis Coderre, other elected politicians, and arts and trade-union leaders marching at the front of a large anti-Israel crowd carrying Hezbollah flags. Hezbollah is a terrorist organization under Canadian law, and to support it is an offence.† Some

*The Conference of Defence Associations, the umbrella organization for military associations, is led in Ottawa by francophones, but until 2006 had no spokespersons in Quebec.

†A Strategic Counsel poll in August 2005—before the Lebanon fighting—found that 81 percent of Canadians favoured deporting or jailing "anyone who publicly supports terrorist bombers." M. Duceppe, the Bloc Québécois leader, argued that he had tried to stop Hezbollah supporters from joining the march and that he had criticized Hezbollah in his remarks. Some other leaders of the parade also subsequently—sort of—disavowed their presence. An Innovative Research Group poll in late August 2006 found that Quebecers were the Canadians least concerned by terror generally and by home-grown terror. The margin of difference between Québécois and other Canadians was substantial.

francophone commentators detected substantial anti-Semitism playing its part in shaping the almost unanimous public response against Israel's "war crimes," including placards reading "Juifs assassins." One writer, Jean Renaud, described Quebec opinion in words that require no translation as "à vomir sur les Israèliens et les Américains." Jacques Brassard, a former Parti Québécois minister, added that he had "toujours été mal à l'aise avec les postures et les lieux communs tiers-mondistes, anti américains, pacifistes et antisionistes" of the separatist movement. Others countered, correctly enough, that pro-peace, anti-Semitic, and anti-American sentiments were not unique to francophones; they did, however, seem more virulent in Quebec in the summer of 2006.* The difference from the Ballistic Missile Defence question was that Prime

*A *Western Standard*/Compas poll of August 6, 2006, asked precise questions and reported that 56 percent of Québécois thought Hezbollah should remain on Canada's terrorist list and that 58 percent agreed it should be illegal to support Hezbollah. When asked if Hezbollah started the war, however, 25 percent agreed and 43 percent disagreed. The same poll, contrary to others, found 51 percent in Quebec agreeing with the government's Mideast policy. There are also signs that Quebec intellectuals are beginning to grow concerned over Islamist intolerance. In October 2006, after Muslims attacked French philosopher Robert Redeker's views, twenty-eight Quebec intellectuals wrote: "Not only do we exhort the French state to take all the measures necessary to apply the constitution on its own soil, we demand that both our levels of government, Ottawa and Quebec City, denounce with force this 'second Rushdie affair.' . . . As for Muslim authorities, we summon them, if they don't want to see the frontal assault predicted, announced, promoted and unleashed by Islamic neo-bolshevism, to dissociate themselves as quickly as possible, with the authors of this 'fatwa,' which they are actively supporting with their silence . . . Resisting totalitarianism and terrorism is not simply putting words on petitions like ours, it's warning criminals in power that we are not afraid and that we will never bend to their barbaric intimidation and liberty-killing efforts."

Minister Stephen Harper presented the Quebec and Canadian public with his reasons for acting as he did. It is only fair to say that large numbers of Québécois did not appear persuaded, but at least Harper showed leadership, in marked contrast to his immediate Liberal predecessors.

Quebec's anti-Americanism is not good for Canada, no more than was its automatic pacifism, anti-militarism, and past opposition to participation in the world wars that threatened Canada's security. Much of Quebec public opinion was on the wrong side of the great struggle for democracy in the Second World War and, in its apathetic response, on the do-nothing side of the Cold War struggle against Communism. Today, many of the province's leaders also seems to be on the wrong side of the defining struggle of our times—that against Islamic fundamentalism.

These positions are also bad for the sovereignists, those like André Boisclair and André Bachand who proudly proclaim Quebec a pacifist nation-in-waiting. It is not my job to advise separatists, but it is blindingly clear to me that American acceptance of a sovereign Quebec is virtually a *sine qua non* if independence is to have any chance of lasting success. Most of the province's business is done with the United States, more than a third of Quebec's gross domestic product depends on that trade, and Quebec tourism and prosperity hinge on good relations across the border. Without American support for Quebec to enter the North American Free Trade Agreement, for example, the new nation's economy would be in serious difficulty, and an independent Quebec, despite much wishful thinking in separatist circles, has no guarantee of automatic adhesion to NAFTA.

Similarly, Quebec's loudly professed disdain for President Bush, American imperialism, the war in Iraq, Ballistic Missile Defence, and its fervid cultural relativism and anti-Americanism are unlikely to ease U.S. concerns about an independent Quebec. Given the fixation in the United States on security after September 11, why should Washington support a pacifist Quebec in any way, shape, or form? Of course, the separatist leaders will ensure that their "foreign policy" pretends to be more accommodating to U.S. security interests in any future referendum campaign, but no one will be fooled. To have a Quebec nation that thinks of itself as avowedly pacifist and profoundly anti-American directly to its north is bound to make Americans even more concerned than they might otherwise be should the Parti Québécois ever succeed in its goal.* Why Duceppe, Boisclair, and the other sovereignists don't realize this point is astonishing. Why the separatists don't realize that Canada's national interests—which include the need to keep the economy growing by maintaining good relations with the United States—apply to Quebec, in or out of Canada, is a mystery to me. How can they fail to realize that an independent, pacifist Quebec will inevitably see Canada, the United States, or both nations assume its defence? Canadian and American national interests will drive this role, and nothing Quebec can do or say will alter this fundamental fact that, ultimately, will leave an independent Quebec without true sovereignty. The disconnect is so great between independentist rhetoric and

*It is only fair to note that both Pierre Trudeau and Jean Chrétien, neither especially pro-American, actively sought U.S. support for a united Canada in the 1980 and 1995 referenda. Behaviour modification in times of crisis works on both federalist and separatist politicians.

reality that, to my mind, it makes everything the separatists say the equivalent of André Boisclair's pipe dreams.

* * *

Quebec's opposition to Canada's role in the conflict in Afghanistan is also the sharpest in Canada, and Prime Minister Stephen Harper faces a difficult task in squaring his support for the war with his political need to win more seats in Quebec and secure a parliamentary majority. Writing in *La Presse* during the early days of the war, Mario Roy saw "an irrepressible current of anti-American hatred manifesting itself here for the past three weeks." By the fall of 2006, 70 percent of Quebecers wanted negotiations with the Taliban, the Strategic Counsel reported from its polling, while 63 percent desired an immediate pullout. Both figures were the highest in the nation. Moreover, Quebec's tolerance for large defence expenditures is limited so long as the alleged fiscal imbalance dominates discussions between the Prime Minister and Premier Jean Charest. Decima Research polling at the end of July 2006 spotted increasing opposition to defence spending in Quebec. All these factors pose serious problems for the Conservative government.

But Harper is a national-interest politician, and, like most English-speaking Canadians, his foreign and defence policy is well ahead of the public mood in Quebec. He will ensure that Quebec gets its full share and more of the contracts his government has pledged to place for the rebuilding of the Canadian Forces. In May 2006 he agreed to implement his election promise to give Quebec a special and permanent post within the Canadian delegation to the United Nations Educational,

Scientific and Cultural Organization, a long-sought goal of the province. This, he said, "symbolizes our vision of a strong, flexible Canadian federation." In return for his largesse, Harper must believe, Quebec's anti-Americanism and opposition to the Afghan War will remain muted enough to allow him to win his majority. Of course, because Quebec premiers of all political stripes always push for more, every prime minister needs to worry that English Canadians will react negatively to major concessions that might allow Quebec a larger say, or increased representation, in foreign policy.

Jean Charest, the Liberal Premier, was delighted that he and the Prime Minister had reached an understanding on UNESCO, and the Quebec Premier has also made it abundantly clear that he has no intention of stopping his push to expand Quebec's role in foreign policy. As he told *L'Express* in July 2006 in an interview during his visit to Paris, the UNESCO arrangement was the first time Ottawa "explicitly recognize[d], in an agreement, the international personality of Quebec, its specificity and its particular role on the world stage." Asymmetrical federalism, which Charest insists has been conceded by the agreement on health-care financing negotiated by the Martin Liberals in September 2004 and in the UNESCO deal with Harper, is "the acceptance of our difference, the unique political personality of Quebec, and the confirmation that our political personality is not the same as that of the other provinces." Sometimes the Quebec *rouges* seem as separatist as the Parti Québécois.

Charest's Quebec has since indicated that it wants to have representatives at the World Health Organization, the Organization for Economic Co-operation and Development, and the World Trade Organization, among other bodies, and the province intends to increase the number of missions it runs abroad beyond the present twenty-eight (with 282 employees at a cost of $350 million a year). As Charest said in Paris: "There is no doubt that we are a people and a nation . . . I see no contradiction in the fact that we, les Québécois, are also Canadians, like the French are French, but also European." Internationally, "we are not subordinate to the federal state. We carry out our business without inhibition and we do not see many limits to our actions" in the fields of health, education, culture, and language—which are, he said, Quebec's fields of competence. There is much in Charest's remarks that many English-speaking Canadians cannot like, not least Foreign Affairs' officials who rail at the "games" Quebec continues to play abroad. The UNESCO role, the *National Post* editorialized, "creates an unfortunate double standard with regard to the provinces, and will undermine Canada's ability to send clear messages about its priorities to other countries."

But if Quebec claims its own particular fields of competence in international relations, then English Canada might perhaps have its own foreign policy as well—notably, a strong international role that goes beyond blue-beret peacekeeping and a defence policy that can support such an activist position. What's good for the francophone provincial goose should be good for the English-speaking national gander. In effect, Louis St. Laurent struck almost that kind of implicit bargain with Quebec in the 1950s. The difference is that, today, a rally against the war in Iraq can put mass demonstrations on the streets of Montreal, and there is no guarantee that Québécois will sit by and acquiesce to a national foreign and defence policy with which large elements of the population, anti-

American and pacifist to the core, disagree. When a battle group from the Van Doos, the Royal 22e Régiment, go to Kandahar in the summer of 2007 in the first large deployment of francophone troops there, Quebec opinion will be tested, as pollster Allan Gregg put it crudely, as soon as "the body bags start coming [back] with the Fleur-de-lis on them." We need to remember, though, that not all Québécois are pacifist. The R22eR are not, and neither are the men and women who volunteer to join the Canadian Forces in large numbers today. When Gregg's prophesy comes true, as it likely will, Quebec's response could be to rally round its soldiers.*

Stephen Harper, consciously or not, has thrown caution to the winds and set out along the path Prime Minister St. Laurent blazed a half-century ago. His Liberal predecessor won Quebec's trust by persuading French Canada that he would do nothing to hurt the province's interests. Harper has begun that process by permitting Quebec to expand its reach in foreign (and domestic) policy and demonstrating that he is a man of his word. With the Liberal Party in Quebec a near-fatal casualty of recurrent scandals, the Conservatives for now appear to be the only federalist party remaining in the field. If they lose this chance to entrench themselves, the Canadian option in Quebec may well be dead, even if the federalism that is now emerging under Harper's direction is a much more pallid version of the one Canadians have known. No one who

*A francophone friend wrote to me privately that "this crap about Quebec not being able to stomach losses to the Van Doos is infuriating. They are not Quebec troops; they are Canadian troops from Quebec. This dangerous tribalism threatens to subvert our national interests, including our security." He is correct.

survived the Meech and Charlottetown discussions on the Constitution wants yet another great debate on federalism, but it is already obvious that if Stephen Harper remains in office, the balance of federal-provincial power will shift away from Ottawa. Much is at stake for the Conservatives in Quebec and for Canada, and Harper has begun to stake out the terms of a new concordat.

It's our war at home and abroad. If Canada is to play its full part, Canadians who believe the issues at stake are vital must demand that the national government retain sufficient powers and expend the resources to meet its responsibilities. Defence and foreign policy are unquestionably federal powers, and Ottawa must continue to exercise them to the fullest extent to advance the nation's interests. Mr. Harper cannot be allowed to forget this fact.

[7]

Multiculturalism and Canadian Foreign Policy

If Québécois sometimes have difficulty in focusing on Canadian or Quebec national interests, their problem is nothing compared with the divided interests and loyalties of the dozens of multicultural communities that make Canada their home. Older and more established groups of immigrants such as Germans and Icelanders were followed after the Second World War by Jews, Italians and Portuguese, Lebanese, and, more recently, Latin and South Americans, Somalis, Indians, Vietnamese, Russians, Koreans, Chinese, and several others. In many Toronto public schools, children from dozens of ethnicities attend class together, all bringing their own particular language to the classroom. Whether or not multiculturalism works as well as its advocates believe, it's unquestionably here, and Canadians need to adapt themselves to its realities.

Michael Adams of Environics, one of Canada's leading polling organizations, has said that multiculturalism is a great success story. Within a decade of their arrival in Canada, he maintains, immigrants' values are essentially the same as those of other Canadians. Newcomers consider Canada's place in the world more important than the old Canadian rivalries of language and region, he goes on, and Canadians are more European in their attitudes than American, more secure in their own culture, and apparently convinced that Canada is not like the United States but uniquely different. John Ralston Saul, "whose writings on Canadians are considered seminal," said the *Washington Post*, observed that Canada "accidentally came up with this post-modern idea of a nation-state, with no dominant group and no dominant ideas . . . You could have a nation of minorities . . . there would be no idea of a majority." I hope Adams is right and I wish he were correct, but nothing in this chapter will support his position. I fear Saul is accurate in saying that Canada has no official culture and that it consists not of two peoples but of many, each with its own identity, all equal one to the others, and with no dominant ideas. Certainly the evidence supports his position.

* * *

Ethnic groups and organizations have always tried to influence Canadian policy, usually with indifferent success. Jews pressed vainly for the federal government to allow refugees from Nazism to come to Canada in the 1930s, for example, while Ukrainian Canadians lobbied Ottawa furiously to gain entry for refugees from Stalinist persecution after 1945. Nonetheless, multiculturalism as an official public policy did not take hold until the beginning of the 1970s, and it was not enshrined in Canadian hearts and minds until the Charter of Rights and

Freedoms became part of the Constitution in 1982. Then it took shape powerfully, and soon it began to exercise substantial influence on Canadian defence and foreign policy.

Consider the Toronto journalist Zuhair Kashmeri, who published a book, *The Gulf Within: Canadian Arabs, Racism and the Gulf War*, in 1991. Kashmeri argued that Canada had failed to consider "the views of its large Arab and Muslim communities before it decided to join the US-sponsored coalition in the Gulf War" that resulted in the liberation of Kuwait from Saddam Hussein's Iraqi invasion. Such action was simply unacceptable to him, and he based his argument on the views of a prominent clergyman, the Reverend Tad Mitsui of the United Church of Canada. Mitsui saw "race involved in judging who is an enemy and who is a friend. For example, Canadians will never think of America as an enemy, and neither can they think of British or the French as enemies . . . But it is so easy to think of Arabs as the enemy. I think this is not fair," Mitsui went on. "Why can't Pakistan be our friend no matter what? Why can't Iraq . . . ? And if you expand that logic, if Canada should exist as a multicultural, multiracial country, you cannot take sides with anybody." Kashmeri then went on to argue that "since multiculturalism advocates celebrating the differences, allowing the traditions and cultures to co-exist, the extension of that policy in foreign policy is a stance of neutrality."

This woolly-headed thinking completely ignores Canada's history, national interests, and continuing need to defend and advance them. What is so striking, nonetheless, is the increasing acceptance of the Kashmeri/Mitsui idea. Yes, Canada participated in the Gulf War of 1991 and, yes, Canada is still in

Afghanistan. But the Chrétien government refused to go into the Iraq War in 2003, arguing for multilateralism to prevail and the writ of the United Nations Security Council to be enforced. In the Israeli war against Hezbollah in July 2006, a Strategic Counsel poll found 77 percent of Canadians believing that Canada should be neutral in this war, even though Hezbollah, the aggressor, had been declared a terrorist organization by Ottawa, and Canada's major activity had been to evacuate citizens from the war zone. Fighting a war against anyone, anywhere, it seems, upsets many in Canadian society, and the best course, therefore, was never—or almost never—to fight. "Traditional peacekeeping"—a Canadian soldier with a blue beret and an unloaded rifle situated between two factions and bringing calm by his very presence—is, in this version of logic, the only acceptable role for the Canadian Forces. UN peacekeeping, it seems, unites almost all segments of a multicultural Canada; fighting a war—except perhaps a war sanctioned by the United Nations—divides them. Multiculturalism trumps national interests, or so some argue.

During the fighting in Lebanon, Prime Minister Stephen Harper took a strong stand against Hezbollah's terrorist attacks on Israel and, by implication, for Israel. The rights or wrongs of the conflict scarcely mattered to the Opposition, much of the media, and the Jewish and Muslim populations. What Harper had done with his condemnation of terror was to abandon Canada's "traditional" honest-broker role, its balanced approach to the Middle East's problems. Balance was more important than standing up to terrorism for Bill Graham, Lloyd Axworthy, the NDP's Alexa McDonough, and others. Anything else would sacrifice Canada's long-standing position as what Opposition leader Graham called a "bridge-builder" of peace in the volatile Middle East.

Many may have shared the idea that Canada should be neutral, but not everyone believed this twaddle that Canada was an honest broker or a major player in the Middle East. The *Globe and Mail*'s Jeffrey Simpson answered one reader's complaints by writing: "You have fallen victim to the false assumption that Canada had much of a reputation for anything in the Middle East. We are bit players there." Simpson was precisely correct. He might have added two things: that, except for the Chrétien era when the government followed a balanced policy, a pro-Israel Canada had scarcely been neutral in its policies towards the Middle East; and, second, that, despite our multicultural community, Canada's national interests do exist. The interests and concerns of the "old country" or co-religionists always seem to take precedence in Canada.

So, how can we explain the wilful blindness of the Kashmeri-Mitsui argument for neutrality as the only acceptable position for a multicultural Canada? I would suggest that the reaction of ethnic groups to such events as the Israeli-Hezbollah conflict and the Canadian Forces' participation in the Gulf or in the Former Yugoslavia might well be explained as a failure of Canada to integrate newcomers into the body politic. We don't teach Canada's history to our children, native-born or immigrant; we say little about our democratic political system; and virtually every Canadian government from John A. Macdonald's to Stephen Harper's has demonstrated remarkable reluctance to explain the country's national interests to the people. If the leaders won't lead, how can the people be expected to understand?

Nor can the established media be counted on to help here. Consider this quotation from the political columnist John Ibbitson of the *Globe and Mail*, who wrote in August 2005 about Canada's new Governor General, Mme Michaëlle Jean. At her press conference the day she was named, Jean spoke about the situation in Haiti, where she was born. Ibbitson wrote that her words were important: "Reflecting a subtle but profound shift in recent Canadian foreign policy priorities, the tsunami of last year, the chaos in Haiti, the exploding troubles in Sudan are not foreign-*aid* issues for Canada, they are foreign-*policy* priorities," he stated, adding due emphasis. "They reflect our demographic transformation, from predominantly European to truly multinational. Problems in India and China and Haiti are *our* problems because India and China and Haiti are *our* motherlands."*

Ibbitson, like Kashmeri before him, fundamentally misunderstands the roots and sources of a nation's defence and foreign policy. He advocates policies of the heart, not policies of the head. He believes that Canadian foreign policy should be based on values and ethnicity, not on national interests. It is understandable that immigrants care about their homeland, of course, but Canada's defence and foreign policy cannot be about loving everyone or even helping everyone. It is not about saying a nation cannot go to war, for example, for fear of offending some group within the country. It cannot be about doing something only to satisfy one or another group's ties to its mother country.

*Lloyd Axworthy has indicated that he shares Ibbitson's approach. In an article in the *Winnipeg Free Press* in August 2006, he wrote that Canada must "track the changing landscape of Canadian society and what it means for the priorities we should set internationally." National interests still apparently count for nothing for this most values-driven former Foreign Minister.

Defence and foreign policy instead must spring from the fundamental bases of a state—its geographical location, its history, its form of government, its economic imperatives, its alliances, and, yes, those who form its population. In other words, national interests are and must be the key.

No nation can do what its citizens of Sri Lankan or Pakistani or Somalian or Jewish or Muslim or Ukrainian origin want—all the time. No nation can do what its provinces, or founding peoples, or some of them want—all the time. A nation must do what its national interests determine it must. Our national interests are long lived. Canada might go to war, and it has fought wars, to protect those interests.

But we have also gone to war for ethnicity. Let us be honest enough to admit that, in 1914, the British connection shaped the Canadian war effort, not national interests. Yes, Canada was a colony and bound by the British declaration of war. But the size of Canada's contribution was driven by the determination of the government and the English-speaking Canadian public to be British, to be part of the Empire, and to accept the burdens, glory, and death of a British war. In the Second World War, after the Statute of Westminster of 1931 won Canada independence in foreign policy, Canada was no longer a colony, but we used this new power to postpone our declaration for only one week after Britain went to war against Germany on September 3, 1939. Were Canada's national interests threatened in 1939? The United States certainly did not think its interests were, nor did any independent state in the Western Hemisphere. Was Canadian unity not endangered by the war? Of course it was. Canadians went to war in 1939 because Britain did, because English-speaking Canadians wanted to support the mother country. Few of them cared what francophone Quebec thought or wanted.

Certainly Prime Minister King, who did understand the issue, handled the strains on national unity far better than Borden had a quarter-century before, and King's government constructed a vast war effort that did its full share in defeating the monstrous Nazi regime. No one should doubt that Canadian national interests were ultimately threatened in the 1939–45 war. Yet every Canadian historian knows that French Canada's version of those events is far different and that the Second World War stands high on the long list of issues where English Canada forced its will on francophone Quebec against the desires of its people. Opinion polls during the war made it clear that Quebecers took a different view of the war from English-speaking Canadians, and not just on the subject of military conscription. Almost always forgotten is the fact that other ethnic groups, such as the German and Ukrainian Canadians, also solidly voted no against conscription in the 1942 plebiscite. The Second World War, like the Great War, was, in Canadian terms, a British ethnic war in which everyone else was dragged along.

But Canada grew up as a nation and began to recognize its own national interests. In August 1940, after Dunkirk and the fall of France made the survival of Britain doubtful, Canada struck its first defence arrangement with the United States because the government recognized that Britain could no longer be counted on to defend Canada. Canadians continued their defence relations with the United States after 1945 because of the threat posed by the Soviet Union. Canada went into the North Atlantic Treaty Organization in 1949, into

Korea in 1950, and into the North American Air Defence Command in 1957–58 for the same reason. Canada's national interests had come to the fore. Ethnicity seemed to be very secondary. But it wasn't, or at least not for very long—certainly not among Canada's ethnic groups.

There are far too many examples. In June 1985 Sikhs blew up an airliner, in support of an independent Kalistan on the subcontinent. This mass murder of 329 people apparently was plotted by Canadians on Canadian soil. It stands as a cautionary tale about the importation of a homeland conflict to Canada and of the utter inability of the Canadian government to respond before terror struck or, as shocking, to resolve the matter in the courts after the fact. Similarly, Canadian Sri Lankans continued unchecked for more than a decade to raise money and to try to buy weapons for the Tamil Tigers, which, finally, have been labelled a terrorist group by the Harper government.

And consider this case. During the collapse of the Former Yugoslavia into warring ethnicities in the 1990s, Serb and Croat Canadians got into scuffles on the streets of Toronto, raised funds for the Old Country, and returned to Serbia or Croatia in considerable numbers to lend their political and military muscle to the bloody, genocidal struggles that killed hundreds of thousands of people there. One Serb Canadian from Edmonton, Nicholas Ribic, was sentenced to three years in jail in September 2005 for taking United Nations peacekeepers—including a Canadian—hostage in Serbia in May 1995. Clearly, Canada had failed to integrate these people into its nationality.

Carol Off, in her book *The Ghosts of Medak Pocket*, wrote of the quarter-million Croats who had arrived in Canada from the 1960s on. "Their continuing identity as Croats was powerful—and much encouraged by the Canadian government," she said. "In 1971 Canada declared itself officially multicultural; and Ottawa began to offer millions of dollars to ethnic communities in Canada to preserve their immigrant identities, a well-meaning policy that unfortunately exacerbated the problem of the angry émigrés who weren't even trying to fit into the society of their adopted country." That was, of course, true for more than Croats. The government, Off goes on, funded language schools and folklore centres—and also, as it turned out, publications disseminating radical nationalist and right-wing messages. What Ottawa did not do was try to make Canadians out of them. Off continues by delineating the pro-Nazi Ustache connections among Canadian Croats and the extraordinary fact that the very idea of an independent Croatian nation, including part of Bosnia, was born at the Norval Community Centre, set up by Croatian Canadians in southern Ontario.

This community centre became the heart of Gojko Susak territory. An Ottawa restaurant owner and house painter when Franjo Tudjman took over the government of Croatia in 1990, Susak heeded his leader's call for the Croatian diaspora to come home. He quickly became a provocateur, literally firing what Off calls "the first shot" in the Croatian war for independence from Belgrade. Soon he was Croatia's defence minister. He used his connections in Canada to raise money for Croatia, up to $200 million, Off suggests, for weapons and aid. Susak eventually presided over the "ethnic cleansing" of Serbs in the Medak Pocket—where Canadian soldiers, trying to prevent the slaughter of Serbian women, children, and old men, killed

Croats in a large pitched battle. It is fair to say that Susak was a war criminal, and, if he had not died before the creation of the International Criminal Court, he would almost certainly have been tried.

The point of the Croatian events is that Canada completely failed to turn Susak into a Canadian. He had arrived here in 1969 and lived in Canada for more than two decades, but his allegiance was to Croatia first, last, and always. Was he any different from the Sikh terrorists? The Tamils? The Palestinians? The Irish? Or the other ethnic Canadians who send money for political purposes, or for guns, to their ancestral homelands? Why has Canada failed to impress its values on the hearts of those to whom it gave shelter and citizenship? Why does the link of "blood and soil" remain so strong? And the key question: Why won't the people who live here give their first allegiance to Canada and its national interests?

In early 1939 a young civil servant, Norman Robertson of the Department of External Affairs, had the task of working out what was to be done about German pro-Nazi Bundists and Italian Fascisti groups in Canada in the event of war. He proposed that the government make full use of the law to block the import of seditious, disloyal, or scurrilous propaganda. He urged the government to refrain from any administrative encouragement by stopping advertising, for example, in suspect newspapers. He called for tax audits of suspected Nazis and Fascists, and for Royal Canadian Mounted Police investigations of applicants for naturalization. In other words, Robertson wanted to use the resources of the state to control anti-Canadian propaganda.

Robertson could be tough (he later prepared the lists of

those Germans and Italians who were to be interned on the outbreak of war), but he knew that toughness was not enough. He wanted to integrate immigrants and make them Canadians. He recommended English classes for newcomers, the provision of social workers and legal aid, access to medical care, the use of the Canadian Broadcasting Corporation's radio programs and National Film Board films to acculturate newcomers, the encouragement of immigrants to join political parties, and the enlistment of churches and other groups into making all who came here Canadians. His goal, he said, was "a positive affirmation of the concept of Canadian Citizenship based on loyalty & domicile and a repudiation of 'blood & soil.'" Robertson was right, but unfortunately his political masters largely ignored his recommendations.

Sixty-eight years later we have still not done what Robertson suggested, or at least not done it very well. The results speak for themselves: a Croat Canadian can become defence minister in Croatia; Canadian Jews pressed Prime Minister Joe Clark in 1979 to move the Canadian Embassy in Israel from Tel Aviv to Jerusalem, whether it made sense or not, and Prime Minister Paul Martin in 2004 to "tilt" towards Israel, while Canadian Muslims argued the reverse; Canadian Ukrainians pressed Brian Mulroney's government to take the lead in supporting an independent Ukraine after the collapse of the Soviet Union, just as those Canadians from the Baltic states did for their former homelands.

These things may be right or wrong in and of themselves; some of them unquestionably are right. They ought to be Canadian policy, however, only if they meet the test of Canada's national interests. They are not good foreign policy if they are done merely to win support from the "padrones" of the ethnic groups who deliver votes during Canadian elections. If we play this game to its logical conclusion, and there is every indication that our politicians are eager to do so, it will become increasingly obvious to Canadians and everyone else that multicultural Canada is completely unable to define and act upon its national interests.

Queen's University political philosopher Will Kymlicka is a leading scholar and proponent of Canadian multiculturalism. He interprets the multicultural ideal as meaning that "the interests and lifestyles of immigrants [were] as worthy of respect (and accommodation) as those of the people descended from the country's original colonists." He has suggested that Canada was lucky in its timing in introducing multiculturalism in the early 1970s when the vast majority of the population was of European origin. Multiculturalism, in effect, was put in place to ensure that bilingualism and biculturalism did not exclude those Canadians who were neither French nor English in heritage. By 1990, when Canada had been changed by a heavy influx of non-white immigrants, the multiculturalism policies were already in place, and the new groups had proven their willingness to work within the framework of a liberal and human rights–based multiculturalism. "To put it paradoxically," Kymlicka says, "multiculturalism has proven to be successful [in] . . . accommodating new non-European immigrants in Canada precisely because it was not initially adopted for such groups." It's luck, not virtue, he says, that made multiculturalism work in Canada.

But has multiculturalism been a success in nation-building, its ultimate purpose, and, if not, can it continue? Did Canada rely too much on the huge and powerful assimilation tendencies of North America to turn immigrants into Canadians? (If only a Somali boy will learn to play hockey, everything will be fine . . .) Has it integrated ethnic communities into the mainstream? Or, with its emphasis on the retention of cultural identities and diversity, has it allowed, even encouraged, emotion-packed minority identities to flourish? Has it forgotten to tell immigrants that this nation is secular, that religion and the state are separate here, and that the laws in Canada are made by Parliament, not God?* Is multiculturalism a celebration, in some ways a masochistic celebration, of nothingness? In other words, does it fail to create a Canadian identity and a sense of allegiance to Canada? Does multiculturalism accentuate differences, intensify antagonisms, divide races and nationalities, and lead to ethnic communities that live separate one from the other and with no ties between them?

Ayaan Hirsi Ali, the Somali-Dutch legislator who fled to exile in the United States in order to escape death threats from her co-religionists because of her views on Islam's treatment of women, has written a stunning book, *The Caged Virgin: An Emancipation Proclamation for Women and Islam.* In it she notes that Dutch multiculturalists (just like Canadians) refuse to classify cultural phenomena as better or worse, only neutral and disparate, and she argues that this liberal blindness actually encourages segregation and perpetuates the grossly unequal

*It is worth recalling that Ontario came within a hair's breadth of accepting a system of shariah law for family disputes in 2004, until the McGuinty government overrode recommendations by the former NDP attorney-general Marion Boyd. When it vetoed her recommendations, the government also eliminated other religion-based dispute settlement tribunals.

position of Muslim women in the Netherlands—and elsewhere. Muslims, she observes, are not the same as the Roman Catholics who won equality in Protestant Holland through a long struggle. The Pope may not favour the idea of women priests, but no pope for generations has opposed the emancipation of women, as Islam still does. To Hirsi Ali, the state must integrate immigrants from the starting point of basic human rights. Either all are equal or none are. Surely she is correct.

Even those who do not usually agree with Naomi Klein will recognize that she, too, was surely right when she wrote in the summer of 2005 in *The Nation* "that the brand of multiculturalism practised in Britain (and France, Germany, Canada . . .) has little to do with genuine equality. It is, instead, a Faustian bargain, struck between vote-seeking politicians and self-appointed community leaders, one that keeps ethnic minorities tucked away in state-funded peripheral ghettoes while the centres of public life remain largely unaffected by seismic shifts in the national ethnic makeup." To me, that is not an unfair description of the Canadian scene.*

Canada needs and want immigrants, and most of us believe that the influx of people from all over the world is good for the country. Certainly I do. But we must make Canadians of those who come here. Recent experience in the Netherlands, France, Britain, and elsewhere suggests that it is not enough to leave immigrants alone, letting them become adapted to

*A series of studies of visible minority immigrants in 2006 reported that Toronto, for example, was a series of segregated communities. "Is there something more Canada can do," said Maraki Sikre Merid, an Ethiopian Canadian and co-author of one of the studies, "to give people a sense of what it means to be Canadian?"

Canada or not as they choose. It is all too likely that some will feel excluded from the mainstream of what they see as a decadent, immoral society and feel compelled to assert their identity, their transnational identity, as Islamists. The reality in Western Europe is that the second and third generation of Muslim citizens are more fiercely Islamist than their parents. At the same time, their sense of themselves as Dutch or British or French citizens, for example, is much less strong than their identity as Muslims. In her book *Londonistan*, Melanie Phillips suggested that the London train bombers differed from most of their contemporaries in only one respect: they were young Muslims who, as Phillips puts it, had "repudiated not just British values but the elementary codes of humanity." The leader of the bombers left behind a video that made it clear he owed allegiance not to Britain but to Islam. Similarly, Geneive Abdo, author of *Mecca and Main Street: Muslim Life in America after 9/11*, has found "alienation from the mainstream of U.S. life, with Muslims in this country choosing their Islamic identity over their American one." Do her findings apply in Canada? In fact, as University of Toronto sociologist Jeffrey Reitz notes, "it is striking that indications of lack of integration into Canadian society are so significant for the Canadian second-born generation [of visible minorities], since it is this group which is regarded as the harbinger of the future."

We may not be in a war against Islam, wrote the American military writer Ralph Peters, "but the extreme believers within Islam are convinced that they are soldiers in a religious war against us." When Muslim leaders in organizations such as the Canadian Arab Federation or the Canadian Islamic Congress argue that the key to checking extremism in their communities is for Canada to change its foreign policies, one must wonder. But that's not how we change policy in the West. Organize, mobilize, campaign, yes, and change government, if you can. Nothing else is acceptable.

We must encourage immigrants, Muslims and all others too, to adapt to these norms. We need to make it clear to those we choose to admit to Canada that we are a nation with national interests, that we are a formed society with values and ways of governing ourselves that have been shaped over centuries, and that, if they wish to come here to join our national project, they must accept these facts of life. Certainly that is what Canadians want: a Strategic Counsel poll in August 2005 showed 69 percent wanting immigrants to integrate into Canada, and only 20 percent saying that immigrants should maintain their own identity and culture. These results were echoed by an Innovative Research Group sounding in November 2005.* The Canadian Muslim Union, a new progressive organization, understands the reality of Canada. Canadian life, Niaz Salini, the group's president, said, includes gender equality, freedom of speech, and gay rights. "These are the values of Canada. You have to accept you're living in a secular democracy. At the same time, you cannot spit on your faith." In other words, the individual can live his or her own life as desired, but the values of the whole society must be respected.

It also needs to be said bluntly to immigrants and the native-born that Canada is a part of Western civilization, with all its many faults and all its enormous successes. We are a product

*Environics contrarily reported in November 2006 that 49 percent believed that immigrant and ethnic communities should be free to maintain their cultural and religious traditions.

of the Judeo-Christian heritage and of the civilization fostered by Greece, Rome, France, Britain, and the Enlightenment's humanistic traditions. Canada is a secular, pluralist, free, and democratic nation whose liberal values are shared throughout the West. These are basic core values. Religion does not determine our politics, individuals can choose their own path, and the rule of the majority prevails. Canadians do not want these things to change, nor should they. While immigrants from non-Western parts of the world have been, are, and must be welcomed, those who wish to come here need to understand that they are not arriving in a piece of vacant territory in flux, one where anything goes. No one need fear practising his own religion (or not), eating her own foods, or wearing her own form of dress in Canada. But changes in the Canadian way of life can only be brought about by majoritarian consensus. It is not, and never will be, permissible to try to force religion on the non-believers, or to practise female circumcision, or to beat spouses, for example, because these things were always done in the Old Country.* Changes in rights and freedoms in Canada can evolve—and have—but that is ordinarily a gradual process. Some things cannot change, however, and rights such as freedom of speech, freedom of religion, freedom from religion, equality, democracy, and the rule of law are inviolate.

In other words, immigrants should come here because they want to join Canada for its freedom and because they agree to accept certain not-very-onerous obligations. That freedom includes the right to assimilate completely, partially, or not

*Environics in November 2006 found that 81 percent of Canadians believed ethnic minorities should adapt to mainstream beliefs on women's issues.

at all, as each individual decides. This freedom is why almost every immigrant who arrived in this new world in the last half-millennium came here. The obligations include accepting Canadian society for what it already is. Immigrants need to make (and need encouragement to make) an effort to learn one of the official languages, the history and culture, and the values of the existing Canadian nation. They need to give Canada their loyalty. For its part, Canada needs to give immigrants the means to be Canadian and to succeed in building a good life here, not simply and implicitly to advise them that they can stay separate. It is becoming increasingly obvious that the racial and cultural separation permitted (and encouraged) by multiculturalist theory and practice in Canada is not good for the future of Canadian society.

Moreover, we are not merely a community of communities, to use poor, benighted Joe Clark's phrase. Canada might be made up of ethnic, linguistic, regional, and religious groups, but it is also a nation with a history of doing great deeds in the past and the strong belief that it can do great deeds in the future. That is the usual definition of a nation. Canada always represented a chance to begin again and to secure a better life for future generations. It remains so—and Canadians have been willing to fight to keep it this way. They still are.

Yes, Canada wants to let all peoples flourish here, but the government and Canadians must insist that immigrants recognize the basic fact that Canada has its own national interests and will seek to further them. They must strongly encourage immigrants to accept the values of our society, the values of Western civilization, the values of Canada, all of which, heaven knows, are broad enough to accommodate a wide range of behaviours. (Our values can and do change, of course—multiculturalism, for example, was not even a glimmer in the mind of Canadians until the late 1960s.) It's easy to pat ourselves on our collective backs and proclaim that Canadian multiculturalism is far more successful than British or Dutch or French multiculturalism. We couldn't have filmmakers assassinated on the street for making the films they choose, we say; we couldn't have subway bombings or riots and car burnings. Yet I know of no evidence whatsoever to suggest that Canada's multiculturalism is much better at truly integrating immigrant groups into the broader society than the British, French, or Dutch models.*

Writing in the *New York Times Magazine* on August 14, 2005, David Rieff said (and I have substituted the words "Canada" and "Canadian" in his text for "Europe" and "European") that "the multicultural fantasy in Canada . . . was that, in due course, assuming that the proper resources were committed and benevolence deployed, Islamic and other immigrants would eventually become liberals. As it's said, they would come to 'accept' the values of their new countries. It was never clear how this vision was supposed to coexist with multiculturalism's other main assumption, which was that group identity should be maintained. But by now that question is largely academic: the Canadian vision of multiculturalism, in all its simultaneous good will and self-congratulation, is no longer sustainable.

*I will say, however, that most of the young, those who have gone through our urban public school systems, seem remarkably colour blind and tolerant of diversity. Whether that applies to the increasing numbers of those educated in madrassas, Hebrew schools, and Christian fundamentalist schools, I do not know.

And most Canadians know it. What they don't know is what to do next."

After the arrest of seventeen young Muslim men in Toronto on terrorism charges in June 2006, after the arrest of Canadian-based Tamil Tiger–supporters trying to buy surface-to-air missiles with $1 million in August 2006, what to do next simply must be at the forefront of government and public thinking. Considering the problem now is the very least we can do. If we don't, the backlash will be terrible when it comes.

Most Canadians want multiculturalism to work. Most recognize that if we can make it a success, if our citizens of every origin can accept Canada's national interests and values, add some of their own traditions to them over time, and become integrated into the polity, then Canada can become a multi-hued nation with a huge advantage in trade, foreign policy, and even defence.* But to make multiculturalism work, Canada needs its leaders to lead, to speak the truth, and to help integrate those who come here into our society. Among other things, that means not pandering to minority communities by twisting Canadian foreign policy into knots in an effort to snare votes in the next election.

I believe that understanding our national interests is the way to shape Canadian foreign policy—a better way than bowing before opinion polls and ethnic pols, a better way than—*pace* Ibbitson—looking for new motherlands. We have only one

*One example: Afghan Canadians, at least fifteen, volunteered to work as translators with the Canadian Forces in Kandahar in 2006. "These guys are all volunteers," one Defence official said. "They're civil servants, civilian employees of DND." An Afghan Canadian added, "It makes them feel good to do something for their country—for both of their countries."

motherland now: Canada. Our foreign policy must be based on what is important to Canadians as a whole—their national interests—not to Canadians wearing only their Old Country/ethnicity/religious hat. Anything else is a recipe for fragmentation, division, and discord and a guarantee that, if there is another war sometime in the future against country X or Y or Z, many "hyphenated" Canadians will be locked up as enemy aliens or supporters. The Charter of Rights and Freedoms notwithstanding, they will be locked up to meet the demands of a frightened public.

It may be entirely appropriate that Canada, as Zuhair Kashmeri would prefer, be neutral in all or almost all wars. But not on the grounds he suggests: that a multicultural nation cannot go to war. Neutrality is and should be an option for Canada—but only if neutrality serves our national interests.

We all want Canadians to care for and about the world, to be idealistic. We all want our compassionate values to be served. Canadians want to help in tsunami and hurricane relief and to help clean up Port-au-Prince. But such things are not national interest issues; they are values issues. They are foreign-aid issues, not foreign policies. They are important, but they are not, for Canada as a nation-state, life or death issues. Those are the national interest issues—security, unity, economics, democracy, and freedom—that must drive our foreign and defence policy. It will help greatly if we can make the distinction and if reporters, especially columnists as experienced and influential as John Ibbitson, can learn the difference.

I began this section with foolish quotes from two journalists. Let me conclude it with the comments of the almost always sensible James Travers of the *Toronto Star* in mid-July 2005 and of Jeffrey Simpson a year later. Travers wrote that "Paul Martin's government . . . must send a zero-tolerance message to those who bring a new country the troubles that make it so attractive to leave an old one. This isn't racism or cultural insensitivity. It is a categorical rejection of bombs, guns and hatreds as legitimate expressions of political will." Simpson answered a query from a reader in an online *Globe and Mail* posting by writing similarly: "A pluralistic country such as Canada, with so many ethnic groups within it, should not allow the ancient grievances imported to our shores by any groups to influence our foreign policy. Those grievances—grounded or otherwise—should be buried or dealt with somewhere else, not here." Some, he went on, have made the Armenian genocide of ninety years ago a way of galvanizing Armenian nationality. "Fine. That's their nationality and cause, not ours—not in a pluralistic country. And I apply the same test to every other miserable dispute that washes into our shores, be it Serb-Croat, Tamil-Sinhalese, Indian-Pakistani etc., etc. It doesn't end, especially if, as the Prime Minister is doing, we begin to play ethnic politics." Simpson's last line was, I suspect, a reference to Prime Minister Harper, who quickly demonstrated in his first six months in office that, by issuing totally insincere apologies for the historic grievances of Chinese Canadians over the hundred-year-old head tax, he was as adept at playing ethnic politics as all his predecessors, Liberal or Conservative.

The truth is that pandering to multiculturalism is a core value of the Conservative Party—and the Liberal Party, the New Democratic Party, and sometimes even of the Bloc Québécois. Michael Adams may argue that immigrants assimilate in a decade, but someone should tell the political parties that everyone has merged into the Canadian persona. None of them act as if Canada was anything other than a collection of ethnicities, and no party leader, no prime minister in my adulthood, has not played the multicultural game. But prime ministers must lead nationally, and they must look after the national interest first and everything else second. They must think about more than the present moment. They must lead.

* * *

I want Canada to be open to immigrants from all over the world. The open door is one of the glories of this country. I want us to be open to refugees too—helping those under attack is a human duty and also something Canada accepted when it signed the 1951 United Nations Convention Relating to the Status of Refugees.

But, in our own national interest, we need to recognize that some people who wish to do us harm or to attack our friends may seek to base themselves here. No one should be allowed to immigrate to Canada without being subjected to security screening, and sufficient resources need to be dedicated to achieve this end. As a minimum, given that Pakistan and Afghanistan are hotbeds of Islamist doctrine, all immigrants from those nations must be thoroughly vetted before admission. In July 2006 the deputy director of the Canadian Security Intelligence Service testified before a Senate committee that his agency has screened only one in ten of the 20,000 immigrants who have come from this region in the last five years. The same care also needs to be exercised with Sri Lankan refugee claimants—Canada has admitted far more than any other country, and the Tamil Tigers' main overseas base of support, not surprisingly, is here. American politicians and officials know about this support, point to "South Toronto" as a terrorist breeding ground, and denounce Canada's "liberal" immigration and refugee policies. When every issue south of the border is scrutinized through the microscope of security, such attitudes do not help Canada get what it wants and needs in Washington.

Similarly, it is wrong for well-meaning Canadians to call unthinkingly for Canada to open its doors wide to every refugee who makes it to Canada. Not everyone who claims to be a refugee is one. People fleeing persecution are; those seeking greater economic opportunity or medical care here are not. The latter groups may well be people we need in Canada, but they should be allowed to enter only by way of the regular immigrant doorways.

Moreover, our citizenship system needs serious review. In 1993 a parliamentary committee considered a variety of questions around citizenship and produced a report; the Chrétien and Martin governments, however, took no action. It is long past time for a new Citizenship Act to replace the legislation that came into effect in 1977. And it may be that a Royal Commission on the Rights and Obligations of Canadian Citizenship should be a precursor to new legislation.

Such an impartial examination also should look at Canada's practice of permitting dual citizenship or triple or quadruple or more—there is effectively no limit on the number of different national passports a Canadian can hold. Before 1977, Canadians who acquired another nation's citizenship, except by marriage, lost their Canadian status. Until 1973, Canada required those who wanted its citizenship to renounce their former allegiance. The 1993 House of Commons committee questioned the meaning of loyalty where people held dual or multiple citizenships and suggested that permitting a Canadian to hold more than one nation's passport devalued the meaning of our own. The committee, in fact, recommended that an adult Canadian who voluntarily acquired another country's citizenship should cease to be a Canadian citizen. There are at least four million foreign-born Canadians with dual citizenship, wrote columnist Andrew Coyne, and an unknown number of the Canadian-born. No one knows how many Canadian dual citizens live abroad. It would be a major, wrenching change to eliminate dual citizenship, as the 1993 committee recommended.

Was the committee correct? Frankly, it is extremely difficult to decide. There are obvious advantages to Canada from its dual citizens in a globalized economy where millions of people travel each year, live and work abroad, or carry on business in different parts of the world on a daily basis. We all benefit from having citizens who can understand the customs of another nation and move our trade smoothly through the bureaucracy in India, the Middle East, France, or Britain. But is there still a downside to this practice, as the committee suggested? Mme Jean, the present Governor General, held both French and Canadian citizenship and gave up her French identity only on being named to her post. When that was revealed after her nomination, it created a few rough moments for her in the media and the public. A royal commission might well consider if Canadians should be permitted—or even encouraged—to hold, as Ottawa's Department of Citizenship and Immigration's website puts it, "two or more citizenships and allegiances at the same time."

Whether individuals can have two or more allegiances simultaneously may be doubtful, and several serious questions about dual citizenship need to be explored. Should Italian Canadians, for example, be allowed as Canadian citizens to vote for and elect representatives in the Italian parliament, as occurred in 2006? Italy created expatriate voting rights, and a Canadian was elected to the Italian parliament; control of the Senate, in fact, changed because of the votes of Italians abroad.* As Sheila Copps, the former Liberal minister, wondered, what will happen when a Canadian with Chinese citizenships gets elected "to China's parliament with a mandate to build up military capacity against Taiwan"? Far-fetched? she asked. "Not if other countries follow Italy's example."

There are far more onerous obligations that can fall on dual citizens abroad. Syria and Iran, to cite two examples, consider that their citizenship is irrevocable, no matter that someone might carry a Canadian passport. What is Canada's position on this issue? Do we expect our embassies and consulates to make representations on behalf of dual citizens who get into legal difficulties in the country of their birth, especially if they entered Iran using an Iranian passport? If they get into difficulty, as some have, Canada can do nothing except make the usual ineffectual representations. Would Ottawa listen any more closely to Iranian representations if a dual citizen of Iran and Canada broke Canadian law?

*Not everyone in Italy was pleased at this result. The day after the election, *L'Unita* noted: "It seems impossible but the fate of this 2006 election has been decided by Italian émigrés of the second and third generation rather than by any people in Italy—by men and women who were not born in their native land and, in the great majority of cases, have never lived there." Consider the response here if expatriate Canadians—or Canadian passport holders, wherever they lived and whether or not they had ever been in Canada—decided the next federal election.

In a world full of choices, should those living here or abroad be made to decide on their nationality? The Chrétien government forced Conrad Black to choose between his Canadian citizenship and his place in the House of Lords. Lord Black chose the House of Lords. No one in Ottawa, however, forced the same choice on the Somali Canadians who returned to Somalia to serve in its interim government or support its rival opposition groupings or on the Italian Canadian elected to Italy's legislature. The Supreme Court has held that there are some government jobs that are open only to Canadian citizens. That seems reasonable, just as it does to say some cultural industries must be Canadian controlled. How do dual or triple citizens fit into this categorization? If an Italian Canadian can vote in an Italian election, why can a British Canadian not sit in the House of Lords and still be Canadian? Why could an American Canadian not control a cultural industry? These things too need to be studied, and perhaps some elemental fairness could be injected into Ottawa's practices in regulating who can sit or not sit in a foreign legislative body.

And what are the obligations of citizenship? Should these not be described and accepted by those to whom we grant citizenship? At the moment, the only requirements are that an applicant for Canadian citizenship be reasonably fluent in English or French and able to answer a few simple questions about Canadian history, geography, and the country's political system. Is this sufficient? We all know Canadian citizens who cannot speak or understand either of the official languages, and many, including most of the native born, would not be able to answer the general knowledge questions. Historically, we expected Canadians to be willing to serve in the military in wartime to defend our territory and our freedoms, and Canada imposed conscription in the two world wars to enforce this demand. Is that still a reasonable expectation?

Should Canadian citizens be able to serve in foreign militaries? Many Canadians of Israeli origin return to Israel to do military service there. Others volunteer for the U.S. forces, and there are Canadians serving in the British, Australian, and French forces. Should their Canadian citizenship permit this service at all or might it only forbid participation in combat?

And what do we do when someone returns "home," as a few of Serb and Croat origin did during the wars in the 1990s, and takes the field in action against Canadian soldiers trying to stop ethnic cleansing? If one of those militiamen killed a Canadian soldier, is this murder or simply an accident of war? Do Canadians turn a blind eye to such behaviour? In an age of increasing ethnic violence and terrorism, such questions need to be closely examined by a royal commission.

What are the obligations of government to citizens abroad? Does Canada owe them access to our health-care system, even though most have paid no taxes to Ottawa or the provincial governments? To the lower university fees available to citizens? To a passport that lets them travel almost everywhere without visas and with minimal hassle?

Above all, does Canada owe all its citizens abroad safe refuge? The Israeli-Hezbollah conflict of July 2006 brought this question to the fore when more than 40,000 Canadian citizens in Lebanon registered with the Embassy in Beirut and became eligible for evacuation by Canada. The Harper government, a half-world away and with scant diplomatic and no military assets at all in the area, struggled to improvise a response and, in fact, did so with substantial success. Almost fifteen thousand Canadians were evacuated to safety in Turkey and Cyprus and then flown to Canada at government expense—approximately $94 million in total.

It turned out, however, that many of the putative Canadians had lived in Lebanon for decades, their only link to this country being their passports. (Almost half of those evacuated returned to Lebanon once a shaky peace took hold between Hezbollah and the Israelis.) Rasha Solti wrote in the *Globe and Mail:* "I hold a Canadian passport, I was born in Toronto when my parents were students there. I have never gone back. I left at age 2." Ms. Solti's passport was clearly her bolt-hole, renewed every five years only to let her come to Canada if she ever needed to do so. Because she registered at the Embassy in Beirut, she was offered a chance at evacuation. Should she have been? Did Canada owe her anything?

Obviously, the government has some responsibility to assist tourists and visitors who are caught up in a conflict. But what about those who hold this country's passport only for reasons of convenience? Those who renew every five years without ever visiting, let alone living in, Canada? This question too needs careful study, and the Harper government has indicated that it is one that concerns it.* When the Prime Minister suggested such an examination, however, he was predictably attacked by Opposition politicians. The representative of one Lebanese-Canadian association did say that once the present crisis was resolved, it might be worth debating Canada's responsibilities

*The *Globe and Mail* reported on October 19, 2006, that the Department of Citizenship and Immigration "will be reviewing the rights and responsibilities of citizenship" in the upcoming months.

to those residing abroad. The royal commission I suggested should examine this issue too.

No Canadian government or Canadian citizen wants to create categories of citizenship, but perhaps there is another way to handle the matter and to stop the use of our passports as a public convenience. In the United States, all Americans, no matter where they live or how many passports they carry, must file an income tax return as a fundamental continuing obligation of citizenship. Essentially, the United States says that those who want to be part of the United States must help to pay for it. Canada imposes no such requirement, though it has tax treaties with many nations. The royal commission I propose might want to examine this approach, because all who write a cheque to the Canada Revenue Agency on April 30 each year are unlikely to be able to forget their Canadian citizenship, no matter where they live. Moreover, should the filing of annual tax returns not be a requirement for adults at home or abroad who are seeking renewal of a Canadian passport?

Such questions are not simply technical matters. Instead, they go to the heart of national identity. Does Canadian citizenship mean something, or is Canada just a hotel that the peoples of the world can check into when it suits them, as novelist Yann Martel famously put it, and check out when their own interests so require? To me, citizenship matters. It is in Canada's national interests that its people owe their allegiance to this nation, understand what allegiance means, and know and accept that there are rights and obligations that come from being Canadian. It is time for the federal government to look seriously at citizenship in all its ramifications.

* * *

The War on Terror involves Canada and Canadians. To say so ought to be obvious. We share the continent with the United States, which was attacked on September 11, and Canadians died in the World Trade Center collapse. The Canada-U.S. border has been greatly affected by the attacks, and the government is spending billions to boost the effectiveness of the security services. Canada has had troops in Afghanistan for six years, fighting a war against al-Qaeda and the Taliban, and Canadian citizens have been arrested for suspected terrorist activities.

Does this activity increase the likelihood of terror attacks on Canadian soil? The answer is unequivocal: yes, it does. Zaynab Khadr, a member of the foremost al-Qaeda family in Canada, told *Maclean's* in July 2006: "Everybody reaps what they plant. If you follow in the footsteps of the Americans, you will reap what they did . . . Violence is not justified," she added, "but it should be expected . . . And should the Canadians expect it with the strategy that's being taken? They should expect it." Despite the general vapidity and cupidity of the Khadrs (who returned here to take advantage of medicare for a son who was wounded fighting the Americans in Afghanistan), this comment is correct: Canadians must expect to be attacked.

But does this danger mean that Canada should opt out of the war against terror? No, not at all. First, the Islamist war is being waged against the West, against democracy, and against secularism, not only against the United States. It is the defining issue of the present era, the struggle of a global medieval theocracy against modernity. As a Western secular democracy, Canada is a target whatever we do, and al-Qaeda had us on its hit list even before Canadian troops went into Afghanistan. Second, and most important, no nation can permit its policies to be determined by terrorists. Pierre Trudeau made that decision for us in October 1970 when he imposed the War Measures Act to counter the Front de libération du Québec. Any Canadian government that caves into terrorist threats should be driven from office; any political party that panders to terror in shaping its policies should be wiped out by the voters. All we can do is to fight against those who try to impose their nihilism on us. Acting harshly against those who try to secure change by violent means is necessary, whether that change is needed or not or "right" or "wrong." A terrorist is not a freedom fighter under another name, and the means employed, not necessarily the ends sought, determine those we must oppose. Stephen Harper understood this. After Hamas won election to power in 2006 in the Palestinian Authority, he cut off aid. Hamas was and is a terrorist organization, and Canada would not give assistance to any such organization.

We need to remember that terrorism is not only an Islamist phenomenon. The most horrific act of terrorism involving Canadians, as we've mentioned already, was the destruction in 1985 of an Air India flight from Toronto by Sikh terrorists apparently based on the West Coast. The Tamil Tigers, Sri Lankan separatists, operated freely in Canada, recruiting and raising large sums of money (mostly tax-deductible!), until the Harper government declared them a terrorist organization in April 2006. The Irish Republican Army and its splinter groups, as well as Ulster Protestant terrorist groups, raised funds for arms in Canada; and Hamas and Hezbollah, terrorist Palestinian groups, similarly recruited and fundraised here, again until they were declared terrorist organizations. Croat and Serbian Canadians raised money for weapons and recruited people to fight in the bloody conflicts that tore Yugoslavia to bits in the 1990s. Our governments turned a near-blind eye to these ethnic-based operations for years, scarcely daring to interfere, hesitant even to stop putting government advertising in the ethnic newspapers, in substantial part because politicians of all parties found it advantageous to shop for votes in ethnic communities. The Liberals were particularly skilled in this regard. When he was Finance Minister in May 2000, Paul Martin even spoke at a dinner organized by a front for the Tamil Tigers, so important were votes from the quarter-million-strong Tamil community in some Toronto constituencies. The only message that kind of foolish behaviour sent to ethnic Canadians was that, as the old song has it, anything goes.

The challenge in fighting terrorism wherever it exists is simultaneously to protect our rights at home. Certainly, some militant mullahs are preaching hate and anti-Semitism in Canada's mosques; in all probability, some foul doctrines are being taught in the madrassas; and the Internet gives disaffected Muslim youth access to a world of bile and hate. But very few Muslims here want anything other than to live and work in peace in Canada. The task of government and the police is to root out all those, like the Khadrs, who are interested in practising terror and, while using the full weight of the law against them, to ensure that the rights and freedoms of the law-abiding vast majority are protected. That requires having moles in the mosques; it demands electronic surveillance of the users of the Internet, e-mail, and chatrooms; and it means having legislation in place to give government the full authority to act quickly and decisively.* But it also means the minimum overt interference with the rights and freedoms of the law-abiding majority. Thus far, the Canadian record has been relatively good in this area—certainly better than those of the United States and Great Britain.

It is not perfect, however. As the O'Connor Report on the Mahar Arar case in September 2006 made devastatingly clear, the RCMP's ability to handle sensitive matters of national security is dubious. United States officials arrested Arar, a Syrian-born Canadian citizen and engineer, at New York's airport and then used information supplied by the Mounties to question him. The Americans deported him to Syria, where, for a year, he suffered torture. As Mr. Justice O'Connor showed, Arar was innocent of any wrongdoing, a fact the Mounties refused to concede as they dissembled to the Liberal government, even after the Syrians freed him. In our national interest, Canadian security agencies need to cooperate with U.S. agencies but must exercise care that facts, not rumours, are passed on. Very simply, the Mounties' bad judgment and poor training in security matters cannot be tolerated by a free society any longer, and the Canadian government needs to ensure that sole responsibility for security questions henceforth rests with the Canadian Security Intelligence Service.

What also must be stated firmly is that existing majority

*One terrorist, Mahmoud Mohammad Issa Mohammad, hijacked an Israeli aircraft in Athens in 1968. He somehow entered Canada in 1987, and the government began deportation proceedings against him the next year. The proceedings still continue, sending a message of legal ineffectiveness that, like the complete collapse of court proceedings against the Sikh terrorists who destroyed a Canadian airplane, can only lend comfort to our enemies.

rights and freedoms must not be sacrificed in a misguided effort at political correctness. For example, editorial cartoons are a bulwark of free speech and a traditional way of expressing opinion, and no one should interfere with the freedom of newspapers to publish them. Libel and hate are not permitted, but comments on religions, religious leaders, and historical figures are allowed. The Danish cartoons that stirred a global controversy in late 2005 were, in fact, tame by most standards of satire, well within acceptable boundaries. The Canadian (and global) Muslim community needs to remember that threats of murder and rioting cannot be condoned because of supposed offence. The leadership of the Canadian media, which, with near-total unanimity (the major exception being the *Western Standard*), demonstrated abject cowardice in caving in to pressure not to publish the cartoons, also needs to remember Western traditions of free speech. Political cowardice, unfortunately, grows directly out of political correctness.

Such cowardice likely emboldens those who would do us violence. The vitriol and hatred of the West, of Christians and Jews, that pours out of the mouths of imams and Muslim leaders every day stirs up fanatics, and this abhorrence reaches into Canada. On June 2, 2006, a combined police operation arrested and charged twelve adults and five juveniles with offences under the country's Anti-Terrorism Act. All were Toronto-area Muslims and some, the charges say, underwent terrorist training north of Toronto. With connections in the United States, Britain, and Pakistan, the group tried to smuggle weapons into Canada and purchased explosive materials to be assembled into truck bombs for use at such sites as the CBC headquarters, the Toronto Stock Exchange, and the Toronto offices of the Canadian Security Intelligence Service. Apparently, there were also plans to seize politicians in Ottawa, including the Prime Minister, and to behead him if Canada did not withdraw immediately from Afghanistan.

None of the charges has yet been proven in court, but what is so striking is, as the director of CSIS noted, "these people were essentially raised in Canada." In other words, whatever efforts Canada made to integrate these men—and in some cases their even more militant wives—into the polity failed. The efforts to teach democracy, to instruct all who live here about the ways in which we settle policy disputes and mobilize support for legitimate ideas, need to be doubled and doubled again. Canadians can no longer assume that democratic ways can be learned by osmosis or that a shallow attachment to our institutions and nationality is acceptable. That lesson ought to have been obvious after the Sikh terrorism of the 1980s, but evidently it has still to be learned by our leaders and by the public.*

Above all, what needs to be made clear to all Canadians is that ethnic politics cannot prevail here. We must be Canadians, not hyphenated Canadians. Dual loyalties, of course, cannot be erased completely, for ethnicity persists through the generations, but attempts to minimize its force must be made along

*So far as I know, no opinion survey has asked Canadians if they believe the values of Islam are compatible with Canadian democracy. In June 2006 the German Marshall Fund of the United States asked Americans and European Union citizens this question—and 56 percent believed these values were not compatible with their own nations' democracy. Among those responding this way, 60 percent said that it was groups within Islam, not Islam itself, which was the concern. The results, accurate to 1 percent given the size of the sample, were published in September as *Transatlantic Trends: Key Findings 2006* (www.transatlantictrends.org).

with extraordinary efforts to encourage those who immigrate to Canada to buy into our society, accept the values of Western civilization, and recognize that Canada's national interests will and must supersede those of their Old Country. That requires education and incentives; it also requires an end to pandering for ethnic votes and the tailoring of Canadian domestic and foreign policies to win them.

Canadian policy must be shaped by our national interests, with our "hard" values of democracy and freedom as its bolsters. So long as our leaders can explain that our interests and key values shape our policies, the majority will give their support. That the so-called hyphen in Muslim- or Lebanese-Canadian has become so important in Canadian foreign policy is because the government has pretended for far too long that Canada has no interests and only "soft" values. Explain the rationale for acting in the national interest, and Canadians will agree.

The Canadian government has a right and a duty, to its citizens and to the international community, to stamp out support for terrorist organizations in Canada and to end both their efforts to raise or launder money and their attempts to buy arms and military equipment. One of the evacuees from Lebanon in July 2006 was a young man who had been sent by his parents to study in Canada and who had acquired citizenship. Interviewed on CBC Radio immediately after his evacuation, he said that he supported Hezbollah, an organization formally labelled as terrorist by Canada (and most of the world), had wanted to fight for it in Lebanon, and how he would support it in Canada. Just rescued from a hell of bombardment and death, his reaction may not have been carefully considered. He is entitled to freedom of speech, but his attitude—if carried into overt action—

is not permissible. Canada has no room for immigrants (and it must have no tolerance for citizens) who actively support Hezbollah, the Tamil Tigers, Hamas, Sikh extremists, the IRA, al-Qaeda, or any of the dozens of global terrorist organizations which blow people up to indicate their support for some irredentist or fanatical religious or secular cause. None. If your cause is terror, you cannot support it from within Canada through membership, money, or lobbying politicians. And if a religious, political, or organizational leader does not disavow the use of terror and violence completely, legislation needs to be in place to deal with him. Never again should a government minister speak at a dinner organized by a front for the Tamil Tigers. Never again should politicians march in a parade where terrorist group flags are carried. Never again should party policies be tailored to win ethnic votes by soft-pedalling the danger posed by terrorist groups here and abroad. Living in Canada as a Canadian forbids all activities that support or condone terror. We are *not* all Hezbollah!

Finally, it is long past time for a Canadian prime minister to tell his people the truth about who and what we are. As one bold leader put it, "Canada has a dominant cultural pattern comprising Judeo-Christian ethics, the progressive spirit of the Enlightenment, and the institutions and values of British political culture. No one should ever downplay the hopes and expectations of Canada's national family. We expect all who come here to make an overriding commitment to Canada, its laws and its democratic values. We expect them to master one of our official languages and we will help them to do so. We want them to learn about our history and heritage. And we expect each unique individual who joins our national journey to enrich it with their loyalty and patriotism." Those words, with a few minor alterations to make them fit the Canadian context, were uttered on Australia Day 2006 by Prime Minister John Howard of Australia, the leader of another of the great immigrant-receiving nations.* Indeed, Australia has a higher proportion of foreign-born residents (22 percent) than Canada (18 percent).

Howard knows that he is in a war for the soul and survival of Australia. The war against Western civilization is a war against Canada's freedoms and all of us too, and I await a Canadian prime minister with the courage to make the same speech to his people.

*Some observers believe that Australia, though it has a smaller population than Canada, has a larger role and standing in the world. After one visit there in the fall of 2005, I am inclined to agree. The Aussies know who and what they are and, try as I might, I could not find them doing the familiar Canadian agonizing over their identity.

[8]

The Foreign and Defence Policies Canada Needs—and a More Hopeful Scenario

In an online discussion on the *Globe and Mail*'s website on July 27, 2006, columnist Jeffrey Simpson spoke hard truths to a reader who bemoaned what he viewed as Canada's breach of its neutrality in the Middle East by siding with Israel. What about our honest-broker reputation? the reader asked. "We are bit players there," Simpson bluntly replied, "and, since the removal of Canadian blue hats from the area, even more itsy-bitsy than before. It is a regrettable conceit of Canadians that (a) they are influential everywhere, and (b) are so highly regarded everywhere that the world is waiting for us to act or pronounce ourselves. Both assumptions are often false, especially in the Middle East." There was a refreshing realism there, a tough-mindedness that is too often absent from the Canadian media and from the nation's political discourse.

Simpson was right. Canada matters today only in the minds of its own people. In the capitals of the world, in the debates in the UN Security Council, in the meetings of the G-8, the World Bank, or the World Trade Organization, Canada is a bit player. Canadian morality is strong, but since Brian Mulroney left power in 1993, nothing else about Canada carries any weight in the world. Unlike his immediate disengaged predecessors and successors, by sheer force of will Mulroney made himself and Canada matter in global affairs. (I didn't expect ever to say such words, but they are correct!)

No one should be surprised at this present Canadian disinterest and disengagement. Obsessed with domestic concerns and a huge national debt, successive governments have slashed the budgets of the Department of Foreign Affairs and International Trade, the Canadian International Development Agency, and the Canadian Forces. If your diplomacy, your foreign aid, and your armed forces are weak and are perceived as such by your friends and enemies abroad, your influence slips. Morality doesn't count in calculating power and influence, nor does political rhetoric. For fifteen years, almost all we have had is a thin gruel of pious rhetoric and inaction. There was almost no sign that the Canadian public wanted anything better. Certainly there was no sign the electorate was willing to pay more for the tools that might have won Canada real influence.

I have argued in this book that Canadians need to shake themselves awake and bolster both their capabilities and their will. We live in a dangerous world, and our naïveté and optimism, buttressed by a visceral anti-Americanism, are all that are left to protect us. These characteristics, we hope, tell those who might hurt us that we are really not like our neighbours, however much we may appear to be. Our anti-Americanism is a disease, a virus that has spread so deeply into the body politic that it threatens—at last—to anger the nation on whom Canada depends for its economic viability and its defence. As one of the senior diplomats at the Canadian Embassy in Washington wrote in his farewell dispatch from the U.S. capital at the end of September 2006, "our economic prosperity . . . and arguably, our destiny depend on access to the American market." He is absolutely correct, and our automatic reflex of anti-Americanism is madness. Government policy must begin to drain this abscess that poisons our political and national life. The Liberals, becoming each day more like the New Democratic Party and the Bloc Québécois in their foreign and defence policies, clearly won't tackle this challenge; indeed, they propose to wallow in detestation of the United States. The Conservatives, if they ever secure a majority government, might. But time will tell.

Managing the Canadian relationship with the United States is critical for this country—for all the obvious reasons of propinquity, shared values, trade, investment, and defence. The relationship's success largely determines Canada's influence in the world. We have to realize that the only nations that will be pleased with us if we fall out with our neighbours are not the countries with which we want to have good relations. We can disagree with Washington and will always do so on specific issues. But we must be friends with the United States in our own national interest. And, as Hugh Segal said a few years back, "no matter who is in the White House, or what the balance is in the Congress or Senate, the relationship with the Americans is always better when our capacity to pull our own weight, deploy in alliance or joint operations, and maintain a diplomatic *amicus curiae* position, whenever possible, is actively advanced."

That is good sense, based as it is on a profound understanding of Canada's national interests, and it is a pity that most of our recent governments haven't followed it. Instead, most Canadians and too many of their leaders prattle about their values and say, loudly, that peacekeeping is what we do in the world—except that we don't. Only a few dozen Canadians serve on badly run and weakly led United Nations peacekeeping operations. The bulk of our troops overseas are fighting terrorists in peace-enforcement missions or wars. Somehow Canadians don't understand this reality, except when a soldier's coffin returns home. Then the public response is first to grieve and then to argue that we should not be fighting at all, or to march in parades glorifying the terrorists who threaten the world. The War on Terror is our war, Canada's war, and one of the main tasks of the government is to ensure that the Canadian people understand that fact.

We praise our multiculturalism as a model to the world, but we do no more to integrate newcomers than we have done to make the Québécois part of Canada. Both new immigrants, flying their Old Country flags, and pacifist French Canadians have a near-stranglehold on the making of Canada's foreign and defence policies. When Prime Minister Stephen Harper spoke out against Hezbollah, certifiably a terrorist organization, polls in Quebec showed an instant and substantial decline in support for his party, and Lebanese Canadians and others marched in Montreal and Toronto under signs proclaiming "We are all Hezbollah." It is illegal in Canada to support a terrorist organization, but the police and the government pretended that they saw nothing, and no one acted against the placard-carriers. Toughening up Canada's security policies and the agencies that implement them still has a long way to go. So too does the necessity to make Canadian citizenship mean something. Those who live their lives here in this favoured land owe their allegiance first and only to Canada.

The conflicts in the Middle East obviously arouse passionate concern here. It is legitimate to criticize Israel, and yet not be labelled anti-Semitic. Similarly, Arab misdeeds can be pointed out without attacks on Islam. Canadians can judge when politicians or editorialists go too far, and they can also assess—and should also recognize—when politicians and the media forget that Canada has its own national interests to protect. Not Israel's, not Lebanon's, certainly not Hezbollah's, but Canada's. It is this country that must be foremost in the minds of Canadians. Politicians and party leaders especially need to remember this priority.

Somehow Canadians and their governments have become blind to the protection of the country's national interests. It is a national interest to keep the country united, but government policies permit and encourage divisiveness. It is an interest to enhance the strength of the Canadian economy, but we piss on the United States, the greatest source of our wealth and the ultimate defender of our country, at every opportunity. It is a national interest to be sovereign and to protect our own people and territory, but we have allowed the Canadian Forces to decay to such an extent that the United States in its own national interest might someday soon need to take over the defence of its northern frontier—whether we like it or not. And Canadians scarcely realize that the Arctic, an area of untold riches facing major foreign challenges, is unpeopled and unprotected.

If they are to survive as a nation, Canadians need to rethink their policies. Happily, there have been some signs that this process has begun. The Martin Liberal government issued an International Policy Statement in 2005 that looked realistically at the globe and talked—for the first time in many years—of Canada as a nation with interests to advance and protect. The Martin government also recognized that the condition of the Canadian Forces was deplorable, and it pledged money to begin the military's renewal. Characteristically for a weak, confused Prime Minister and government, the bulk of the promised funding was supposed to be provided in years four and five of a five-year plan. That was a pledge no weak minority government could credibly make. Stephen Harper's Conservative Party won the election in January 2006, and it committed itself to maintaining the Liberal pledges—and, indeed, adding to them.

Even so, it was jam tomorrow, with more money in the future, but too little today. The first Tory budget did offer a ritual nod to the election promise of $5.3 billion to be added to the Department of National Defence base budget by 2011, the same five-year horizon the Liberals employed. But in the next two years, 2007 and 2008, the planning time frame used for virtually every other measure in the federal budget, there was only $1.1 billion in new money going to the Canadian Forces. That paltry increase is simply not enough even to begin to rebuild and rearm the nation's military. As the Chief of the Defence Staff, General Rick Hillier, said in the autumn of 2006 (with extraordinary bluntness even for this outspoken senior officer), the Canadian Forces were "still very much on life support systems" after "a decade of darkness" where "all of our focus" was "designed to constrain, reduce, close, get rid of, stop doing, or minimize."

Finance Minister Jim Flaherty said in his 2006 budget speech that the government promised to implement its "Canada First" defence plan to strengthen the nation's "independent capacity to defend our national sovereignty and security. Realizing this vision," he continued, "will require large-scale investments in every region of the country to strengthen the Canadian Forces." There were, however, very few details.

Many were very critical of the new government's first budget. But, in June 2006, some flesh was put onto the bare bones of the military in a week of extraordinary announcements about defence equipment. On Monday, it was $2.9 billion for three Joint Support Ships for the navy. On Tuesday, the army heard that it would get 2,300 medium trucks at a cost of $1.2 billion. The next day, it was medium- to heavy-lift helicopters, at least sixteen of them, for $4.7 billion; and on Thursday, $8.3 billion worth of strategic (C-17) and tactical (C-130J) lift aircraft. The total was $17.2 billion, a good week's work for the military, and extraordinarily quick work by the Conservative government. In less than five months in office, the Harper government had moved decisively to meet the most pressing requirements of the Canadian Forces.

The equipment was genuinely needed. The army's trucks, for example, were more than twenty years old and cost more, most sources agree, in ongoing maintenance than they are worth. The new vehicles, besides creating manufacturing jobs in Canada, will save the Canadian Forces money that can be used for other purposes than trying to keep old clunkers on the road.

The air force's present thirty-two C-130 Hercules are also over-used and costly to keep flying. Getting seventeen new C-130Js will provide tactical lift into the future, allow the retirement of the oldest Hercs, and, with the four C-17s also being purchased, give Canada at last a capacity to respond to major domestic crises without needing to beg the United States Air Force for heavy lift—an earthquake in British Columbia or an ice storm in Montreal, to cite just two possibilities. The C-17s will add capabilities to the Canadian Forces as well, giving the military a strategic flexibility it has never before had. Moreover, getting the new aircraft will allow the Canadian Forces to operate fewer aircraft more efficiently—thereby producing some personnel and maintenance savings. It might also be possible to rent the heavy-lift aircraft to other nations, breaking the Ukrainians' control of the heavy-lift rental market.

Similarly, the helicopters and the Joint Support Ships will meet pressing needs. The Chinook helicopters—the government is reportedly trying to acquire some from the United States for Afghan service—will replace those Canada stupidly sold to the Dutch a decade ago, and for which we have paid the price ever since. The support ships will replace the navy's two ancient replenishment ships and add a roll-on/roll-off capacity as well as the ability to transport a company and a half of soldiers.

But the Canadian Forces still have requirements that must be met if Canada is, truly, to rebuild its military capacity. The military needs a big-gun armoured vehicle, preferably tracked, to replace the old 1970s vintage Leopard tanks and the cancelled Stryker Mobile Gun System. I think the continuing utility of heavy armour to the Canadian Forces became obvious to soldiers in the Kandahar operations,* and in September 2006 the government decided to send a squadron of Leopards and troopers from Lord Strathcona's Horse to fight with the Task Force there. If the armour operates effectively in Kandahar's villages, the case for a new main battle tank will be made. At the same time, the artillery needs more new guns, and the Chinook helicopters on order will be much more useful if there are some Apache helicopter gunships to protect them in operations. Apaches might be more effective in providing close air support for Canadian troops than the six CF-18 jets the government seemed to be preparing for deployment in the autumn of 2006.

The Joint Support Ships, while a huge improvement over those we have at present, cannot transport the personnel or the equipment required to deploy a complete battle group abroad. Only what General Hillier called "a big honking ship" can project force abroad, and, ideally, the navy should have two or three of those vessels. We won't get that many, but even one will be a vast improvement over the present situation. Such ships, able to carry helicopters and up to 800 troops each, if protected by naval task groups (and they must be), could give the nation the ability to deploy and operate an integrated force effectively almost anywhere in reach of the sea. Ships like the United States Navy's *San Antonio* class would fit the bill and, politically important in Canada, they do not look like aircraft carriers. (In the 2004 election, Prime Minister Paul

*"If you'd asked me five months ago, 'Do you need tanks to fight insurgents?' I would have said, 'No you're nuts,'" said Lt.-Col. Omer Lavoie, Commanding Officer of the Royal Canadian Regiment Battle Group in Kandahar in September 2006. "But . . . they're acting more like a conventional enemy."

Martin scored points against the Conservatives' defence policy by charging that Stephen Harper wanted to get Canada into the carrier business. It was nonsense, but the memory lingers on, and a *San Antonio* vessel type, the navy's preferred choice, would carry helicopters but not resemble a carrier.)

The navy also needs ships, both armed vessels and icebreakers, that can operate on the approaches to, and in, the Arctic Archipelago. They must be part of a concerted plan to exercise sovereignty in the North, a plan to ensure that Canada can hold what it has against the challenges that are certain to come as the ice melts. General Hillier's reorganization of the country's defences, and especially the creation of a tri-service integrated Canada Command charged with the defence of the homeland, is a first step in the right direction. Canada's "home game," as the new Chief of Land Staff, Lieutenant-General Andrew Leslie, called it, must be one we do not lose.

Our "away game," abroad, is vitally important and much more expensive in dollar costs. General Hillier has talked of concentrating Canadian efforts overseas to gain credit from our allies and to get Canada a seat at the table where decisions are made. In the Former Yugoslavia, where Hillier served in the 1990s, Canada received no say, something that clearly still grates on his nerves. "We can offer our government more options to pile on in such a way that we get the profile and we get the credit for it." Profile matters because it creates influence, and influence helps a nation get its way in the world. Canada will get more influence if it is present in large numbers in one place than if its troops are located in penny packets in a dozen locations. One supply line is also easier to maintain for the under-strength, under-equipped Canadian Forces.

General Hillier has also reorganized the military's ability to respond abroad, giving it a long-needed focus on operational effectiveness. He led the International Security Assistance Force in Afghanistan when he was the army commander, and, as Chief of the Defence Staff, he pushed for the expanded commitment to Kandahar in 2006. The general captured the public's attention when he described terrorists everywhere as "detestable murderers and scumbags" and charged the Canadian Forces with helping Canada's allies root them out. "The possibilities of taking casualties are always there," Hillier said in July 2005. "I do think there needs to be an awareness across Canada that we're in a dangerous business." Later, he spoke about the risks: "We are soldiers. This is our profession. This is who we are and what we do."

He was right. The casualties fighting the Taliban in Afghanistan have been hard to bear, especially with public opinion in Canada so anxious over the toll in lives and deperate for a quick-fix solution that is simply not available. The enemy has been strong enough that the government's and the Canadian Forces' commitment to the 3-D approach of defence, development, and diplomacy has not been able to receive a fair trial. When troops are fighting to establish security, the efforts at reconstruction that involve the RCMP, diplomats from Foreign Affairs, and development experts from the Canadian International Development Agency, along with the military, necessarily get pushed to the backburner. The efforts go on (and $106.5 million will be spent in 2006 and a similar amount in 2007), but they are constrained by the tactical situation that has often forced Provincial Reconstruction Team members to hunker down in guarded compounds instead of helping the Afghan people.

As a result, the reconstruction team achievements after almost a year of operations in Kandahar seemed minimal. One commentator, Commodore (Ret'd) Eric Lerhe, called the 3-D effort "largely fiction," and he noted that the Canadian International Development Agency lagged badly in its efforts and that several important Canadian non-governmental organizations refuse to participate in 3-D work because they don't want to cooperate with the military. Thus, there were few highlights. One was that the ten RCMP officers with the Canadian reconstruction team in Kandahar helped to train the Afghan National Police (including women police officers) and, using Canadian funds, built two police stations, provided twelve police trucks, supplied a wide range of police equipment from traffic pylons to handcuffs, and paid for a local tailor to make one thousand uniforms for the Afghan police. In addition, local mechanics were found and hired to maintain the vehicles, thus creating a few good jobs in a country without many of them.

Other Canadians helped the Kandahar fire department, assisted thousands of refugees to return to their homes, gave medical care and installed new wells in villages, distributed school kits donated by Canadians, and provided computers to Kandahar University and to the provincial governor so he could communicate with Kabul. Officers attended innumerable *shuras*, the meetings with local elders that fill a large role in local governance. All such activities operate under the overall protection of infantry (and their numbers had to be increased in September 2006), but one Canadian officer was badly injured when attacked by an axe-wielding Afghan militant at one village meeting. No one seemed to be trying to find alternative crops (or a controlled market) for the opium-growing farmers (reported to be more than 12 percent of the Afghan population), an essential task if the grip of local drug lords, at least as dangerous as the Taliban, is to be broken. The reconstruction team's work is a start, but there is a long way to go.

Less well known than the Provincial Reconstruction Team is the Strategic Advisory Team—Afghanistan, an aid project worked out by President Hamid Karzai and Canadian military commanders. Some fifteen advisers, most drawn from the Canadian Forces, work directly with Afghan government ministries in Kabul to assist with the planning of and accountability for the Afghan National Development Strategy. This plan will become the basic strategic economic document for the country's future because it will articulate objectives and develop the plans to implement them. The overall time frame for success in Afghanistan is said to be ten to twenty years, but no one knows if Canadians could remain that long. However, Canadian soldiers did serve in NATO Europe for more than forty years and in Cyprus for three decades.

There is one additional effect from the Afghan conflict. Operating initially under U.S. command but now serving in a NATO-led force, the soldiers have seen enough combat to become blooded—a terrible, old-fashioned, but not wholly inappropriate word. They have learned as their great-grandfathers and grandfathers did in the two world wars and in Korea that well-trained soldiers can fight and survive and that a unit can sustain casualties and continue to function. That costly but priceless lesson is essential for every army to learn. For an army that had done only peacekeeping and peace-enforcement for the last two generations, not that this service was without killings, ethnic cleaning, post-traumatic stress, and other human costs, this shift in focus was important if the warrior ethos was to be reborn and reclaimed in the army. The idea that Canadians wore only blue berets also had to be knocked out of the military mindset, where it existed almost as much as in the public mind. No one ever publicly stated such a fact, but this goal was almost certainly part of Hillier's plan. To quote General Leslie, the military had become "completely and utterly risk averse. We have been consumed by bureaucratic efficiency, and become fixated on process and planning." Combat and a concentration on effectiveness in operations will knock some of those walls down.

But General Hillier has done more in the transformation of the military. The newly established Canadian Expeditionary Force Command will lead and mount operations overseas, something that will become far easier when the staff shakes down and gets into gear, and when the promised new equipment and additional personnel come on board. With enhanced Special Operations forces including a larger JTF-2, the Canadian Force's elite Tier 1 unit, a Canadian Special Operations Regiment now ready for deployment (that will, in fact, have dispatched some soldiers to Afghanistan before the end of 2007), a Command to lead these special forces, and a renewed airborne capability, the Canadian Forces should be able to fight Afghanistan-type conflicts and credibly claim to be able to defend Canada. Moreover, Hillier has created a Standing Contingency Task Force, a rapidly deployable integrated army-navy-air unit that had its first major training exercise in November 2006.

The overall emphasis on operations is clear, and when the new structure is functioning efficiently, the Canadian Forces will be able to conduct two operations at once, one of Afghanistan scale and the other slightly smaller. Simultaneously, Hillier says, the Canadian Forces will be able to run maritime and air operations. While all this is under way, the army is reorganizing the reserve into Territorial Defence Battalions, eventually to be twelve in number; and the regular army's "teeth" will consist of nine permanently affiliated battle groups based on the existing infantry battalions. This organization should be able to defend Canada and operate abroad in Afghan-type conflicts.

But will that be all the Canadian Forces can do? What must be remembered—and there are voices at National Defence Headquarters saying it has been neglected—is that not every future Canadian war will be fought in failed states in land-locked Asian (Afghanistan) or African (Congo and Darfur) regions. Afghanistan, for example, is a traditional war against insurgents, an old-fashioned war, and not at all a struggle against a well-equipped enemy with a panoply of modern weaponry. There are many states with such arms, and not all of them are friendly.

Some officers see Hillier and his young staff—the "Hillier Youth," they are called derisively—as creating a cult of personality; others label General Leslie "the boy general" and worry about his single-minded enthusiasms. The point is that some see the transformation of the Canadian Forces into a military geared up for Afghan-type wars as one that drains the lifeblood from the air force and weakens the navy. Is the air force destined only to carry troops (a "trash hauler," cynics call it) or to get new fighters and a close support capability in the future? Will Canada at last sign on to Ballistic Missile Defence and continue to press for a NORAD with a wider mandate than at present? Is the navy to focus on defending the Canadian coasts or will it get the "Single Class Surface Combatant" ships it wants to replace the Halifax-class frigates a decade hence? Will it keep its submarine capacity, something most sailors (who recall how much time they spent in the Persian Gulf tracking Iran's three obsolete Kilo-class submarines) think is essential? Will the politicians recognize that the country's shipyards must be put on a "continuous build program" that keeps expertise and technology in place to build some sixteen to eighteen ships over the next two decades? Or will it be the same old tap-on, tap-off lack of foresight and planning that wastes dollars and resources? Everyone except the army lives in trepidation, and there is some realism in this view—if the Afghan experience alone is driving the reshaping of the military. The kind of force structure Hillier's Canadian Forces create will, unless we are careful, determine the very few things Canada can do.

Flexibility in planning must be the key, and a realistic assessment of the future strategic environment requires that a small nation such as Canada keep all its options open. Is the 3-D approach workable or have the difficulties in fully implementing it in Afghanistan made it a questionable strategy for Canada to use in operations within failed states? Are major wars a possibility in the next five, ten, or twenty years? If so, where? Will we always operate as part of an alliance? How credible are military threats to Canadian territory? The Canadian Forces appear to be operating on the assumption that there will be no major military threat for at least two decades. Is that reasonable or rational? Will we continue to use our effective, efficient navy, limited as it is in number of ships, to play a role projecting power abroad? How can we maximize defence cooperation with the United

States while maintaining the utmost sovereign control over our nation's airspace and sea approaches and the Canadian military? How can the Canadian Forces cope with major terrorist attacks in Canada and in a world of terror and proliferating weapons of mass destruction abroad? Are the Canadian Forces prepared for a catastrophic natural disaster on Canadian soil? Such questions, and not only Afghan-type scenarios, need to be considered and planned for. Choosing niches now and rigidly planning for them means casualties in the future.

Above all, the services need more soldiers, sailors, and airmen and women. With a nominal strength of just above 60,000 and an effective strength of 53,000, with reserves of about 25,000 all told, the Canadian Forces need the Harper government to meet its pledges to add 13,000 regulars and 10,000 reservists—quickly. In an era of nearly full employment and an aging population, this total will not be easy to get. It's not that casualties will slow recruiting—there is already growing evidence that the reverse is true and that the prospect of action will attract adventurous types who might have been turned off by their prospects in an ill-equipped, under-strength peacekeeping military. The difficulty is in the demographics, with an aging population and much of the potential youth coming from recent immigrants who are not culturally attuned to military service. The reserves, especially the militia and the navy, have had success in Toronto, Montreal, and Vancouver in reaching multicultural Canadians; the regular forces have not, leading General Hillier to suggest that citizenship be given to immigrants who volunteer and that the Canadian Forces relax background checks on applicants. Already 68 percent of CF personnel are over thirty years of age and 34 percent are over forty; the median age of all recruits is twenty-five; and the median age of soldiers serving abroad is thirty-one. Today, Canada's military may be the oldest in NATO, and that is certain to cause the Canadian Forces difficulties.

The problem of numbers will be made even worse by the pending retirement or resignation of ten to fifteen thousand members of the military in the next several years. These are the technicians and trainers, the warrants and the majors, who make the military function. How they can be replaced is problematic at best, and the Canadian Forces' recruiting system, unfortunately, is badly broken. Fixing it—new TV advertisements are only a start—must be Hillier's first task, or none of his plans will come to fruition. Hillier has said that his goal is to enrol 30 percent of applicants in one week and the next 50 percent within a month, though the remaining 20 percent need to be scrutinized closely. Care must be taken before enlistment, with medical, criminal, and security checks and careful screening for drug use. But no longer can it take up to one year to enlist a recruit, nor can the training system continue to have recruits waiting months to get their basic and trades training. At Canadian Forces Base Wainwright, the new and highly advanced Manoeuvre Training Centre is well equipped to prepare soldiers for deployment; the shortfalls in the training system lie at the initial and preparatory phases of military life and in the shortages of officers and non-commissioned members to do the training. New deployments overseas (to Lebanon or Darfur, which the NDP's Jack Layton said he would support if Canada got out of Afghanistan) will make it impossible to have enough trainers on the ground in Canada. With a generation of officers and non-commissioned members getting battle experience in Afghanistan, the leaders will be in place. The only question is whether they will have the trained soldiers to lead.

There is one other key priority: fixing the procurement system. With so many departments and agencies involved in defence purchasing, with billions at stake and regional interests demanding their cut, with inter-service disputes pitting one environment against the others, every defence purchase has turned into a slow march to obsolescence. It can take more than fifteen years to get a ship from the drawing board to sea. It can take just as long to get a helicopter from a production line to the pilots who will fly it. This timeline is completely unacceptable, especially when Canadians are at war. A powerful new agency, reporting to the defence minister, needs to be put in place to overcome departmental, regional, and service rivalries. The Canadian Forces can't wait until 2020 to get new equipment and to overcome the obsolescence and decay that still traps it. To its credit, the government has indicated that it is accelerating the process.

What is certain is that, without more troops and without new equipment, Canada will be unable to do anything else abroad so long as the Afghan commitment continues. To sustain 2,500 soldiers in Afghanistan demands almost the full resources of the overstretched army and air force. Once the new recruits come into the system, the officers and non-commissioned members required to train them cannot be deployed. In other words, there is a three- to five-year period ahead in which Canada's ability to deploy to a new theatre of operations, either combat or blue-beret peacekeeping, will be strictly limited. Only the navy can deploy for the foreseeable future.

Still, the Harper government and General Hillier's military have unquestionably taken several steps in the right direction.

The one caveat is that Canadians have been promised military reform in the past, only to see the contracts ripped up. The infamous EH-101 Cormorant helicopter deal, tossed aside by Jean Chrétien in his first days in office in 1993, is the most recent example of partisanship trumping defence needs. Paper promises do not always translate into boots on the ground, ships at sea, or aircraft overhead. It could happen again, not least because the Conservative government is in a minority position, with all three Opposition parties soft on defence. Governments are elected domestically, and defence priorities are usually not vote-getters. Those who believe that defence matters need to keep the pressure on the government.

Remember that Paul Martin's ill-starred government also made huge promises of money for the Canadian Forces. The Harper minority government cannot promise spending measures five years ahead with any more confidence than the Liberals did. The Conservative government genuinely might wish to improve the condition and fighting abilities of the Canadian Forces, but wishes are worthless without political will and the funding to implement them. The debilitating uncertainty over the future roles, capabilities, and equipment of the Canadian Forces will continue to sap the military's strength.

But I remain an optimist. The land is strong, as a Trudeau Liberal election slogan once said, and Canadians have always responded to good leadership. They can be brought to understand and support the steps necessary to protect and advance their national interests.

All that has been missing for decades past is vision and leadership—and a few great national projects that can unite and inspire all Canadians, both the immigrant and the native-born.

Could Canada not develop the resolve and the technologies to clean up its own water and then take them to Africa? Could the prime minister not approach the president with a credible, carefully costed plan to clean up the Great Lakes? Could we not find the cure for AIDS and give generic drugs to the world? Could Canadians not end their own blight of child poverty and work to eliminate it everywhere? Such ideas could be effective in fostering a sense of true Canadian citizenship and, when exported, help in eliminating a few of the root causes of terror. We have a long way to go, but maybe, just maybe, we can begin the journey in the next decade. If we can do so, then the bleak scenario with which I began this book can be revised.

* * *

Tuesday, February 11, 2015 It was 7:32 in the morning when the first light quake rippled through a Vancouver that was just getting itself together to go to work. It was raining, and the thunderstorms were almost certainly loud enough for only a few to notice the tremor. The hosts of one popular morning television show saw their coffee jiggle, and they made a brief, joking mention of it before carrying on their discussion of the city's newest high-end restaurant on Robson Street.

But eighteen minutes later, a 5.2 earthquake on the Richter scale shook the city, knocking pictures off the wall, swaying the Lions Gate Bridge, and rocking the freighters in English Bay and the pleasure craft in the city's many marinas. A few cracks appeared in Pender Street's pavement, where just minutes before the surface had been smooth. Mothers looked at their children across the breakfast table and wondered if they should drive them to school or take them down to the basement to huddle in a corner. The TV hosts seemed more than slightly rattled this time, and the picture jumped on tens of thousands of TV sets, but the city was used to such seismic events. Those driving across the bridge from North Vancouver fretted that the wet, swaying roadway might delay their long commute even more.

They had no reason to worry about being late for work; everyone was going to miss work this day. At 8:08 a.m. the long-feared "big one" hit Vancouver. An 8.9 quake, more than a thousand times greater than the previous one, rumbled through the area. The impressive bridge across the Lions Gate fell into the water, taking hundreds of cars and thousands of people with it. Buildings in the business core, mainly the older ones, shuddered and rocked as their electric power went down and the water and gas lines burst. Fires began to spread through the basements and up to the higher floors. Cheaply constructed condominiums on English Bay fell apart and roads buckled. A great crevice opened up on Cambie Street. A few cars and drivers fell into the pit almost unnoticed as everyone else scrambled for safety, trying desperately to stay upright on what had suddenly become a liquid sidewalk. Buildings constructed on landfill almost disappeared as the earth quickly turned to the consistency of thick soup. Vancouver's airport became completely unusable in the space of seconds. The CBC, CTV, Global, and all the private television channels went off the air; almost all the radio stations disappeared into silence as the electric power supplying the region cut out. A rocky avalanche roared down Grouse Mountain in North Vancouver, smashing everything before it, cutting roadways and Highway 99, and rolling over houses.

The Mayor of Vancouver, eating breakfast at home when the quake struck, died when his condo crumbled in the shock. The Chief of Police was on his way to headquarters when the Lions Gate Bridge collapsed beneath him. His deputy tried to reach him, then stepped forward and attempted to take control of the growing chaos. Most members of his force, except for the morning shift that was taking over from the late-night shift, were scattered throughout the city and its suburbs. No one had any idea of the casualties so far, but as the fires took hold and as panic spread, the police, fire departments, and the few still-functioning hospitals knew there would be more than they could handle. Many of the emergency personnel deserted their posts, desperate to find out what had happened to their families.

What no one yet fully realized was that the quake had hit more than the Vancouver area. The Juan de Fuca Plate, stretching all the way from the Queen Charlotte Islands to California, had rubbed together with the North American Plate, and the earthquake that resulted wreaked havoc through Washington state and Oregon. Portland and Seattle, along with Vancouver, were the hardest hit major population centres. Although the seaside cities were spared a tsunami, the coast lowered itself by more than a metre and, in some places near Seattle, the land slid as much as 6 metres seaward. The harbour facilities were almost completely ruined from Portland through to 40 kilometres north of Vancouver. And now, according to a light plane flying between Seattle to Abbotsford, Mount St. Helen's had started to smoke again. The quake, it appeared, had activated the old, shattered volcano.

The first word of the earthquake reached Ottawa about 11:15 a.m. EST. The Government Operations Centre run by

Public Safety and Emergency Preparedness Canada received the initial report, and the duty officer notified his superiors and began calling in representatives of all the departments concerned. Bureaucrats quickly began putting together lists of the resources their departments had available near Vancouver, rightly assuming that their assets in the areas directly affected would not be immediately—if ever—available. The Prime Minister's Office began writing a brief and calming statement for the country's leader to hand to the media.

At National Defence Headquarters, the Minister was just back from visiting Canadian troops in the Arctic, so he asked the Chief of the Defence Staff to provide a list of all the Canadian Forces' military assets in and near British Columbia. There was a good deal. The navy's Pacific Fleet headquarters in Victoria fortunately had survived almost unscathed, and its two Joint Support Ships were in harbour. So, too, were three frigates and four coastal defence vessels, along with a dozen Cormorant helicopters and some of the new Search and Rescue aircraft. There were, perhaps, three thousand sailors. The ratings were quickly put on standby, and the Admiral's staff began planning just how they would use the vessels and the helicopters to ferry sailors—some armed but most with rescue gear—to the mainland. The decision, quickly made, was to send 400 sailors, twenty trucks, and ten bulldozers on the first support ship, and another 400 sailors, including divers, on the next, along with bulldozers, jeeps, and trucks that the roll-on/roll-off vessel could handle easily. All would be on the ground in Vancouver by early evening. The naval reserve ship in Stanley Park, HMCS *Discovery*, Ottawa and Victoria soon learned, had been destroyed in the quake, but planning for emergencies had been raised to a high level, and reserve sailors knew they were to gather as soon as they could at designated schools on the city's outskirts.

The army similarly had added up its assets. A Territorial Defence Battalion Group in Vancouver had been training for six years or so to help "first responders" and to work in Domestic Operations, and the 2,000 reservists in the greater Vancouver area had been given their rendezvous where pre-packed equipment awaited them. In addition, the quick response battalion at Comox and the Engineers school at Canadian Forces Base Chilliwack, reacquired in 2009, both had heavy equipment for training and for emergencies such as an earthquake. There were additional army units at Edmonton, across the Rockies, and aircraft, quickly commandeered from Air Canada and Westjet, began to fly the troops to Abbotsford, the nearest large airport to Vancouver. The air force had only a few patrol aircraft in British Columbia, but its eight C-17 transports (four ordered in 2006 and four more, once their usefulness had been established during the flood year of 2009, picked up second-hand) and its seventeen new C-130J transports at Trenton went on standby. The Disaster Assistance Response Team, based at Kingston, moved to Trenton at once and, with two C-17s at its disposal, had its hospital and water-treatment operation up and beginning to run on the outskirts of Vancouver by noon on Friday. The rest of the air force's transports began hauling personnel and supplies west, and the Hercules dropped substantial amounts of food and water by parachute to cut-off areas. The army's big 5-ton trucks loaded up with rescue equipment and supplies at the Edmonton base, and the first convoys left early Wednesday morning for the long drive over the Rockies.

The Prime Minister had received her first detailed briefing Tuesday at about the same time as the first military units went on standby. The word from British Columbia was horrifying. Fires were sweeping through large parts of Vancouver, and the breaks in water supplies and the disruption to the fire department's crews made controlling them impossible. There was widespread looting, and the Prime Minister gave orders to the navy and army to shoot if necessary to restore order. Hundreds of people had been confirmed dead, but there were certainly many thousands more. Very few reports had yet reached Ottawa from smaller cities and towns, where there was considerable damage, and the provincial government in Victoria so far had done little but call for help from Ottawa. After hearing this tale of destruction and the immediate lack of resources, the Prime Minister excused herself from the meeting to call her friend, the President of the United States.

When she returned, her demeanour was as calm as usual. "I told him that there were areas in which we could cooperate, and he asked if we could take care of the U.S. towns immediately south of the border. I said I thought we could certainly help in Point Roberts, Washington, and in other towns nearby," the Prime Minister said, "and he promised to get 600,000 MREs (Meals Ready to Eat) into Abbotsford within two days."

Were any of the big Ukrainian or Russian air transports available for charter? one official asked. The Vice-Chief of the Defence Staff replied that this source had already been tried, but the situation in Central Asia and the civil war in the Philippines had absorbed every single one of the aircraft until at least the end of February. "I think we can manage without leasing heavy lift," the Vice-Chief said, "but it will be a real stretch. We'll need to work aircrew to the max, and we'll also need the railroads to carry the heaviest equipment and additional food supplies, water and tents." The Prime Minister thanked the officials for their efforts and went off to speak to the nation on radio and television.

If only this was Canada's sole crisis! While Ottawa struggled to cope with the disaster in British Columbia, two small Islamist terrorist cells in Montreal and Toronto decided to seize the opportunity to strike. They were furious at what they saw as the godless immorality of Canada and horrified by gay marriage, pornography, Canada's continuing participation in the War on Terror, and its friendship with the "Great Satan" to the south. Communicating by e-mail, chatrooms, and cellphones, they agreed to launch their long-planned attacks in the morning rush hours on February 14. But the Combined Anti-Terrorist Squad, beefed up as Muslim rage grew exponentially around the globe and in Canada's cities, had been listening in on the chatter and working with informers in the mosques. Heavily armed tactical units swept the terrorist cells up before any harm was done.

The United States was completely absorbed by the huge disasters in Portland and Seattle, but there were still enough Congressmen in Washington, DC, to note how efficiently the Canadians had nipped the terror plots in the bud. No one demanded that the border be closed or that army or National Guard patrols be mounted on the Canadian frontier.

The earthquake was a horrific disaster, to be sure, leaving thousands dead and dealing a crippling blow to the British Columbian and Canadian economies. Individuals in Vancouver griped about the federal response, but provincial government officials and politicians understood that the Canadian Forces and the federal government had helped to save thousands of lives.

Who had got Canada out of its mess? The government had worked to beef up the armed forces with new equipment and more personnel, and it had invested money in the security services. Fortunately, there had been enough time to put policy changes into practice. A generation of inattention to Canada's defence and security needs had been remedied by hard work and substantial sums of money.

So who deserved the credit? Canada's governments had done the job, and so, too, had those Canadians who elected them. Who was responsible? Canadians. Whose war was it? It was Canada's—and it proved that the war against terror and the ongoing war with a sometimes violent and capricious nature could be won.

Index